To Joanne

AUTHOR
Steve Sweeting

DESIGN
Geraldine Chorley

EDITOR
Peter Carr

DEPUTY EDITOR
Nick Robbins

COVER PHOTOGRAPH
Steve Sweeting

PHOTOGRAPHY
Steve Sweeting/ Brian Phipps/ iStockphoto/ Shutterstock unless otherwise stated

Copyright © 2013 Blaze Publishing Limited/ Steve Sweeting
First published in the UK in 2013 by Blaze Publishing Ltd

British Library Cataloguing-in-Publication Data
A catalogue record for this book is available from the British Library

ISBN: 978-0-9549597-3-9

All rights are reserved. No part of this book may be reproduced, stored in a retrieval system or transmitted in any form or by any means electronic, mechanical, photocopying, recording or otherwise without the express permission of the publishers in writing. The opinions of the writers do not necessarily reflect those of the publishers.

Printed in England by Polestar Wheatons

Blaze Publishing Ltd
Lawrence House, Morrell Street, Leamington Spa, Warwickshire CV32 5SZ
01926 339808/ 01926 470400
info@blazepublishing.co.uk
www.blazepublishing.co.uk

WILD BOAR: A BRITISH PERSPECTIVE

CONTENTS

FOREWORD 10

INTRODUCTION 12

HISTORY OF WILD BOAR IN BRITAIN 14

THE BIOLOGY OF WILD BOAR 34

HUNTING WILD BOAR IN BRITAIN: THE KNOWLEDGE 46

HUNTING WILD BOAR IN BRITAIN: THE EQUIPMENT 68

HUNTING WILD BOAR IN BRITAIN: THE EVENT 88

TALES OF WILD BOAR HUNTS 112

WILD PIGS OF THE WORLD 130

WILD BOAR RECIPES 140

INDEX 144

ABOUT THE AUTHOR 146

ACKNOWLEDGEMENTS 148

FOREWORD

I have known Steve Sweeting for a long time indeed. His fresh approach to hunting, farming and countryside use has always impressed me. His politics lie somewhere to the right of the middle, and he has always held strong feelings on hunting and firearms regulation. Furthermore Steve has never been afraid to voice his opinion, even if it went against contemporary thinking. On every occasion he has done so, his point of view (in my experience) has always been a valid one. He's also been vocal about adding British wild boar to the list of quarry species and introducing legislation that would give the species a close season.

The author has spent much of his life working and hunting in both the United States and Africa. The American influence on Steve is clear to see in his attitude to hunting. A former member of the UK Special Forces, serving with the SAS, his military training is also evident, too. These experiences blended together make Steve's hunting style both unique and refreshing. As a hunting outfitter he specialised in the American market and was a popular annual exhibitor at the SCI convention. His Carminnows Estate in SW Scotland often caused controversy in the national press and on internet forums, but not a bit of it ever bothered Steve. He was forthright about what he offered – ethical trophy collecting, which was the same as many other prestigious deer parks did in England. He had many happy repeat clients who loved to hunt with him in the Glenkens, which is a testament in itself. Steve offered so much more than trophy collecting in his well-maintained deer park, which was, incidentally, 50 per cent forestry and no easy place to shoot deer. His total hunting holdings covered many acres of open hill, forestry and farmland, all providing excellent deer stalking and true free ranging wild boar hunting.

Steve's estate included a working farm, which bred rare breed pigs and wild boar for the specialist meat market. The security of farm stock on the estate was second to none, but Steve was often unfairly blamed for supposed damage caused by boar that had allegedly escaped from his holding. This couldn't have been farther from the truth. Dumfries and Galloway already had a sizeable, but mostly unnoticed, free ranging wild boar population, and some of these were soon attracted to Steve's stock behind the wire. Indeed Steve had a harder time keeping marauding boar out than keeping his own in. Undaunted by unfair criticism, Steve made regular inroads into the wild boar population living feral on his hunting areas, and was ever ready to turn out for any friendly farmer suffering boar damage. His experience in farming and hunting wild boar makes for factual reading, and anyone with an interest in British wild boar will find this book very rewarding. All angles are covered, from the fascinating historical research, to useful chapters on suitable calibres, rifle choice, hunting techniques and recipes, with a fine chapter of boar hunting anecdotes with clients in this country.

As a registered RFD and former military operator Steve's firearms knowledge is immense, and his attitude to safe firearms use is always pressed onto anyone who hunts or shoots under his direction. Likewise the ethical dispatch of all animals hunted by him and clients under his wing is always of paramount concern. However, on the rare occasion a client has pulled a shot, or after an RTA involving deer, Steve is one of the most dedicated guides I have seen on a bloodline following up wounded game. His now ageing black labrador Cleo is mustard at following both boar and deer. She has as soft a mouth on feathered game a handler could wish for, but conversely this lab is absolutely fierce on boar.

This book also includes a short chapter on wild pigs of the world. Steve's African experiences are always bubbling below the surface and I have enjoyed many a safari with him in pursuit of warthog and bushpig. Steve was always a good guy to have around in a tight corner in some far flung corner of Africa, or indeed in any dangerous situation. I have taken part in elephant cropping operations with him, hunted marauding leopard alongside him, wrestled with an impressively sized python that took great offence at my efforts to secure it – much to Steve's amusement, and we've worked together on anti-rhino poaching operations, too.

Steve Sweeting is a regular contributor to Sporting Rifle magazine as an overseas hunting correspondent. His narrative has always been interesting and informative without any added bullshit, but with just the right degree of seriousness and a splash of humour. I have a massive amount of respect for him as a writer, hunter, solider, conservationist, and I am proud to count him as both a trusted colleague and friend.

Peter Carr
Editor-in-chief, *Sporting Rifle*

INTRODUCTION

It has been many years since my first encounter with wild boar, but that first meeting had a profound effect on me and left an impression that has lasted for almost 30 years, during which time these creatures have become an integral part of my life. I have farmed them, hunted them, eaten them and, on occasion, even hand reared them, and yet I never tire of working with them.

Although they are clearly closely related to the domestic pig, an animal that I have also farmed, they are, by nature, a totally different beast. While pigs are greedy, disorderly, overwrought animals, wild boar have a more peaceful persona about them; a calmness and dignity that is in direct contrast to their cousins. Wild boars seem to crave a peaceful life, but in times of trouble they will fight their way out of a tight corner with strength and aggression that belies their otherwise peaceful disposition.

I can fully understand why the wild boar was revered so much by our predecessors the ancient Britons, and why they are so often referred to in historical publications and accounts of mythology alike. Since the dark ages they have been symbolic of ferocity and aggression in battle, generosity and hospitality in the home, as well as being a totem of fertility within a marriage.

It is also understandable why the wild boar, with their fearless nature, became one of the five 'Beasts of the Chase' favoured by our Anglo-Saxon royal households. It was the relentless hunting, along with deforestation and reclamation of land for farming, that led to the demise of wild boar in this country. Until now the UK was the only European country not to have wild boar as part of its wildlife.

I wrote this book for several reasons, not least of which was out of a sense of respect and admiration for these extraordinary creatures that have, in recent years, made a comeback as a free ranging animal in the British countryside after a 700-year absence. Sadly, even in the areas where small, isolated communities have established themselves, they are being pressurised by hunters, farmers and the population at large without any protection in law. It might be argued that given the history of these animals in Great Britain they should have as much protection as our native deer species, as well as all of the non-indigenous deer that have become accepted as part of our rural wildlife.

Compared to other game animals in the UK there have been very few written accounts of wild boar in the English language – Martin Goulding's book being a notable exception, although even his publication pays very little attention to hunting the species. It was my intention to compile an all-encompassing volume that will give the uninformed an insight into these fascinating creatures and the informed, hopefully, an agreeable bit of bedtime reading.

Whether the observer is out shoot a trophy, manage a destructive herd or simply watch and maybe take a photograph or two, there is nothing quite like the adrenalin fuelled excitement of a wild boar suddenly appearing out of the woods and coming into full view.

HISTORY OF WILD BOAR IN BRITAIN

Whether it happened overnight in a cataclysmic explosion, or over decades, possibly centuries, through gradual erosion, the narrow strip of land connecting what is now mainland Europe with Great Britain ceased to exist around 7,000 years ago. Either way, it was an end to traffic passing over the connecting land bridge, but the way it ended would have had a very different impact on the fauna, flora and human population of the day.

In the case of an apocalyptic collapse it would have meant an immediate stop to land based animals migrating between the two land masses, with many casualties in the process. On the other hand, slow erosion would have meant that the diminishing isthmus would have gradually made travel more treacherous with each passing year. As the solid ground gave way to salty marshes, many smaller creatures would have had their journey terminated at the edge of the boggy ground. Larger animals such as bison, elk, deer, wild boar and the small migrant population of human beings would have continued to wade across until even they were stopped by the reclamation of terra firma by the sea.

Human beings of that period had not really changed much for 100,000 years and looked pretty much the same as people do today, only with less expensive haircuts. During this time the climate in Europe had undergone many changes, but by 8,000 BC the last ice age had come to an end and both the sea levels and the temperature were beginning to rise.

During the Mesolithic age the human race eked out a living by subsisting on fruit, nuts, berries, leaves, and of course hunting; this was the time of the hunter-gatherer. These Stone Age inhabitants of Britain had already learned the importance of management in hunting by making sure that their quarry was not over exploited. Dr Francis Pryor, in an overview of his book *From Neolithic to Bronze Age,* refers to evidence that they even enticed wild boar and deer to come to water holes and woodland clearings by laying down food – a first step towards farming.

By 5000BC the human race was using tools, making clothes and jewellery, and using language to communicate with other hunter-gatherers throughout the continent. Then, suddenly, the people who had settled in what is now Britain, having been cut off from the rest of the continent, and numbering just a few thousand individuals, found themselves isolated from the rest of the world. The other early inhabitants of the British Isles, the Celts, Romans, Angles, Saxons, Vikings and Normans would come along later.

Chapter 1 — HISTORY OF WILD BOAR IN BRITAIN

The original Britons lived in caves, crudely cultivated the ground with deer antlers, and used shaped flint as arrow- and spearheads to hunt for the game that had been trapped on this island with them. Strangely, it was noted that after the separation of the two land masses the arrowheads used for hunting became smaller in Britain, and it might have been expected that this isolation would have slowed development on our small island. Presumably, however, the continent was still close enough for the latest technologies to filter across the Channel.

So mankind advanced from the Mesolithic to the Neolithic period; a progression that was defined by a transition from hunter-gatherer to farmer. Small villages began to appear similar to the one that was discovered in 1850 at Skara Brae in the Orkneys, a settlement that was inhabited in about 5000-4500 BC.

Farming was much more like hard work than hunting, but it came about because of the need for a regular and consistent food supply to nourish the inhabitants of the small communes in which people now lived. It also served the need to provide food for the ever increasing population.

However, there was a lot more to farming than simply planting a few seeds and waiting for them to grow. Whereas hunters would blend in to the landscape unnoticed, farmers would change it beyond all recognition. Instead of following the herds of deer and wild boar they settled in convenient and fertile areas and learned to plough whole tracts of land that were first cleared of trees and then sown with primitive food crops. Early settlers would have brought with them the ancestors of sheep, cattle and goats from mainland Europe, and farmers began breeding domestic pigs from the wild boar that flourished in the British woodlands.

New skills did not stop at farming. Neolithic people knew how to tame many of the animals with whom they came into contact and understood how to make these beasts work for them. They were able to skin animals in order to utilise their hides for clothes or leather shoes and they realised that wool could be harvested without killing the sheep.

Religion was also practised, in so far as if a crop was planted it would be reasonable to pay homage to the sun, earth or rain in order to secure a bountiful harvest. In the same way a hunter would want to invoke the spirit of the wild boar or deer in the hope of having a successful hunt. The rest, as they say, is history.

People from all over Europe began to settle in the British Isles, although it should be emphasised that until the Romans came in 55 BC, Britain was simply a geographical entity without politics or any single culture. It could be argued that this remained the position until James I of England (VI of Scotland) established a union between England and Scotland and created a consolidated Britain.

The migration was just a trickle at first, starting with the Beaker people around 1900 BC. They were so called, it would seem, simply because many of the artefacts found associated with these people were – you've guessed it – beakers. As historian Sean Lang pointed out, this is a bit like calling us the 'Tupperware folk'.

It would seem that the Beaker people got on with the Neolithics. They even helped them to build Stonehenge, possibly introduced them to the idea of living in proper round huts instead of caves, and probably, most important of all, showed the Neolithic people how to mix copper with tin to make bronze.

Wild boar's history on the British Isles dates back thousands of years

Chapter 1 — HISTORY OF WILD BOAR IN BRITAIN

THE CELTIC CONNECTION

At around 500 BC the Celts began to arrive from central Europe. It is unlikely that there was ever an organised Celtic invasion because the Celts were a fragmented warring race continually fighting among themselves. They were loosely tied by a common bond of religion, language and culture. Celts were above all else warriors who relished the thrill of the battle and coveted the plunder that could be won as a part of the spoils of war. Not all of the Celtic culture was connected to fighting though; they were also merchants, highly talented artisans, and were responsible for bringing iron working to Britain.

The Celtic races were very religious and ceremoniously buried their dead, quite often with artefacts that were in keeping with their status in life. The grave of a warrior would include items like arrow heads and wild boar tusks; the wild boar being associated with ferocity and courage in battle.

The Celtic people made their own ornaments and jewellery, which were often exchanged for livestock and slaves. Many of these artistic artefacts and coins depicted images of wild animals, including wild boar, which the Celts held in very high esteem.

Paraphernalia associated with war, including helmets, standards and bugles, all had images of wild boar upon them; the animal's symbolic power having a great influence on the warrior's prowess in battle.

The most unlikely Roman conqueror of all, Claudius, recognised the symbolic importance of the wild boar to the Celtic warriors when he sent an army of 40,000 legionnaires to fight Queen Boadicea. An army of this size was unprecedented in Iron Age Britain, but Claudius needed to succeed in taming this outpost on the edge of the known world where Julius Caesar had failed. *Legio Vigesima Valeria Victrix* or the Twentieth Victorious Valerian Legion was one of four legions, probably originally raised by Augustus, that Claudius used in 43 AD to put down the revolt led by the rebel Queen, and they used a running wild boar as their insignia.

The wild boar was largely seen as a male totem by the ancient Celts, not only representing fierceness and bravery in battle, but it was also a symbol of masculinity and sexual prowess. The sow too was seen as an emblem of fertility, abundance and prosperity. In Celtic tradition the animal's magic was all powerful, and talisman, amulets and charms were made out of boar's tusks for protection and good luck.

MYTHS AND LEGENDS

The wild boar was always important to the art and mythology of the Celtic people. It was known to them not only for its ferocity and its cunning nature, but it was also prized for its meat, and as such a feast of any importance would undoubtedly include wild boar as a central offering. Being such a prized meat, the wild boar became a symbol of hospitality, and serving it to a guest demonstrated the honoured status of the recipient – it also proved the tenacity and hunting prowess of the host as well.

The Celts realised that the boar, even with its sharp tusks and ferocious nature, was a shy animal that preferred to avoid human contact; only living up to its fierce reputation when cornered or forced to defend itself or its litter against attack.

Not only was the wild boar once native to Britain, this wild ancestor of the modern pig was here long before the very earliest settlers arrived on our island. It was indigenous to the British Isles long before any of our predecessors were here, which makes it rather sad that by the beginning of the 16th century it had been hunted to extinction. Arrogantly our authorities question whether they should be allowed to be re-introduced.

Boars appear throughout mythology as magical, often destructive beasts. In the Welsh Mabinogi fables, Gwydion tells Math, son of Mathonwy of the arrival of strange creatures from the south called pigs – hobeu – belonging to Pryderi, who got them from Arawn, the King of Annwn, which is the Celtic Otherworld. The hunting of the Otherworld pigs is a favourite theme throughout Celtic mythology.

Otherworld pigs are enchanted beasts that have usually been transformed from humans as a punishment for carrying out some evil deed. In mythological tales the boar is often directly or indirectly responsible for the death of a hero and their appearance in dreams was thought to be premonitory, as in Isolt's forewarning of the death of the great warrior Tristan, a vision of which came to him in a dream of the death of a great boar.

Great importance was attached to the bristles of the boar; perhaps because they are the distinguishing characteristic of the animal, or maybe that they were symbolic of its strength. For example, Fionn MacCumhaill, sometimes referred to as Fion, meaning blonde or light, was a mythical hunter warrior who is said by some to have been killed by stepping on a boar's bristle after breaking a taboo against hunting wild boar. However, it should be said that other accounts claim that he is not dead at all but rather he sleeps in a cave somewhere beneath Ireland and will awake to defend Ireland at a time of great need.

To add further significance to the animal's coat, some of the extraordinary boars that King Arthur fights in the fable Culhwch and Olwen, have bristles that are made of gold or silver.

There are many examples of supernatural beasts throughout Celtic and Welsh mythology with the common characteristic being their unnatural, white colour.

One such story concerns King Arthur who was pursuing a large, white deer, but when he arrived at Sir Pellinore's well, which was known to be a magical site, he no longer had his hunting party or his horse with him; while another tale recalls Pryderi and Manawydan in pursuit of a 'gleaming white boar', which leads them and their dogs to a magical trap.

Fertility and continuation of the clan was a major concern of the Celtic and Welsh peoples and here again, animals – and wild boar in particular – were strongly tied to fertility in Celtic and Druid mythology.

A prosperous tribe was indicated by healthy animals and plentiful hunting; to this end it paid to keep on the right side of the goddess Ardwinna whose constant companion was the boar. Ardwinna was the Celtic version of the Roman goddess Diana.

Celtic and Anglo-Saxon helmets bearing boar-head crests have been found in a number of places; the crests were supposed to give protection to the warrior. Beowulf, in the Anglo-Saxon epic bearing his name, went into battle with a boar-head standard, which was symbolic of his power as a leader.

The most well-known of all legendary boars is Twrch Trwyth. The story of his battles with King Arthur are told in a collection of tales from the Mabinogion, which was translated from the the *Red Book of Hergest* by Lady Charlotte Guest.

In this epic tale, Culhwch seeks to win the hand of his beloved Olwen. The young man is clearly keen on the maiden, but Olwen's father, Ysbaddaden Pencawr, is a forbidding giant who issues Culhwch

Boar emblems and insignia are replete in the history of Britain: from the banners of Roman invaders, to Celtic totems, and the goddess Ardwinna's constant companion

Chapter 1 HISTORY OF WILD BOAR IN BRITAIN

William the Conqueror's arrival in Britain heralded the introduction of boar hunting as sport

with a lengthy list of difficult tasks to fulfil before he can marry. The final tasks are to cut Ysbaddaden's hair and shave off his beard.

The giant's beard was so tough that to soften it Culhwch had to obtain the blood of the Black Witch. As if that was not going to be hard enough, the only thing sharp enough to cut the beard was the tusk of Ysgithyrwn, the wildest, biggest boar in all the land.

After killing this boar, Culhwch enlists the help of his cousin Arthur to get the only scissors and comb up to the task of dealing with the giant's hair. These just happened to be between the ears of Twrch Trwth, formerly an Irish king who had been transformed into an irate boar with poisonous bristles. After causing the death of several of Arthur's men, the boar surrenders the scissors and comb, after which he is driven into the sea off the coast of Cornwall and drowned.

Culhwch proved himself by rising to the task when a lesser man might have given up. He cut the giant's hair and shaved off his beard and then married his beloved Olwen. This just goes to show that a brave heart can and did win the hand of a fair maiden.

It is strange that the fierce imagery that comes up time and again in Celtic folklore depicting the boar as being such a ferocious, cunning beast is so contrary to the animal that we know as being a largely peaceable animal, and one which poses little threat to humans. It is true that many of the stories involve the boar being hunted – a situation in which their strong resolve and aggression would naturally be provoked – perhaps fuelling their feisty image in this period.

Druid folklore tells many more tales some concerning the magician Merlin. After his men are slaughtered in battle, Merlin is driven mad with grief and takes refuge in the forests of Caledonia. It is here that he gains the gift of prophecy, and is later seen running wild with wolves and a wild boar.

The legends and folklore regarding wild boar were prolific in ancient Britain, but they are not solely the domain of pre-history. As late as the 19th century stories abound of a giant wild boar known as the Beast of Dean that roamed the Forest of Dean terrorising villagers.

A ROYAL QUARRY

Hunting has always been enjoyed by the English nobility. Apart from anything else, it provided training for war due to the skills that were required, such as tracking, the use of weapons, horsemanship, and courage; pretty much the same disciplines that were needed for medieval warfare.

Both men and women hunted the variety of game animals found living wild in England, but even in those early medieval times (soon after the collapse of the Roman Empire in western Europe) the chieftains, noblemen, aristocracy and even the church had a say in who was able to hunt or take quarry from common land.

Although the Anglo-Saxon kings were great huntsmen, they never set aside areas that were to be dedicated to hunting. Historians have found no evidence that any of the Anglo-Saxon monarchs (c.500 to 1066) actually created forests, or set aside areas for that purpose. All that changed however after 1066 when William I defeated King Harold at the Battle of Hastings.

In order to ensure the English were suitably subjugated, William introduced the French form of feudalism; took control of the English treasury; imposed harsh laws, including the Forest Laws; and, possibly worst of all, created the *Domesday Book*.

> **By God's Body I would rather that my son should hang than study literature. It behoves the sons of gentlemen to blow horn calls correctly, to hunt skilfully, to train a hawk well and carry it elegantly. But the study of literature should be left to clodhoppers.**
>
> *Anonymous gentleman to Richard Pace in 1517*

The *Domesday Book* was a survey of England compiled under the orders of William. It is thought to have been carried out because of a need for more money. The survey was conducted by commissioners, grouped in about eight teams that travelled from county to county. The teams were led by bishops who questioned inhabitants under oath.

Records, that still exist today, show that over 13,000 towns and villages were surveyed. From the information collected in the *Domesday Book*, harsh taxes were demanded from the English people.

All land belonged to the crown. One quarter was treated by William as personal property and the rest was leased out under strict conditions. The country was split into manors, which were given to barons by the King.

In return the baron and his knights had to serve on the royal Grand Council, pay various dues and provide the King with military service when required. The baron kept as much land as he wished for his own use, then distributed the rest among his knights, who were thereby bound to meet the baron's military needs when either he or the King called for them.

The knights in turn allocated sections of their lands to serfs who had to provide free labour, food and service whenever it was demanded, with or without warning.

As soon as he was crowned King of England, William began introducing strict new laws, and under the new Norman king forest law was widely imposed. The law was primarily designed to 'Protect the venison and the vert'. In other words it was to protect the 'noble animals of the chase', which were, notably: red and fallow deer, roe, and wild boar, as well as the greenery that sustained them.

Forests were designed as hunting areas reserved for the monarchs and their guests. The concept was introduced by the Normans to England in the 11th century and was continued by subsequent monarchs until, at the height of this practice in the late 12th and early 13th centuries, one-third of southern England was designated as royal forest. At one stage in the 12th century, all of Essex was a royal hunting forest, and on his accession to the throne Henry II declared all of Huntingdonshire forest the same.

Before the Norman conquest the kings of England enjoyed the right to hunt freely on their own lands, in much the same way as any other land owner did, or, for that matter, still does today. It was not a privilege of being king, more an advantage of wealth. William the Conqueror changed all that.

In Normandy the strict preservation of game was confined to the aristocracy and following the defeat of England, William saw an opportunity to impose the same restrictions in his new kingdom. William the Conqueror and his sons were notorious in their devotion to hunting. The compiler of the *Anglo-Saxon Chronicle* noted that William: "Preserved the harts and boars and loved the stags as much as if he were their father."

Chapter 1 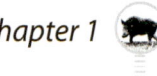 **HISTORY OF WILD BOAR IN BRITAIN**

Similarly, Henry of Huntingdon recorded that he "loved the beasts of the chase as if he were their father." On account of this, in the woodlands reserved for hunting, which he called the 'New Forest', he had villages rooted out and people removed, and made it a habitation for wild beasts.

In medieval times there were an estimated 69 forests. Only the monarch or his servants hunted in the forests. Permission to hunt in forests could also be gained by the granting of a royal licence. The animals subject to the forest law were the red deer, fallow deer, roe deer and the wild boar. Some of the royal forests are still in existence today and they include: the Forest of Dean, Epping Forest and the New Forest. Medieval peasants only had the right to hunt any beast over common land, unless such right had been restricted by some special royal grant.

The strict medieval forest laws reserved the rights of hunting to the ruling class and were hated and resented by the lower classes. Punishments for breaking the laws were severe. Peasants accused of poaching were liable to hanging, castration, blinding or being sewn into a deerskin and then hunted down by ferocious dogs. Although the forest laws and the consequences for breaking them were instated by William I, some historians say that the penalties for breaking those laws were exaggerated by the Anglo-Saxons as a means of propaganda.

Medieval hunting was divided into two different types of hunts: The 'at force' hunt and the 'bow and stable' hunt. The former were the most strenuous forms of hunting and were designed for young, fit and very active men. As the name suggests there were many huntsmen involved who arranged themselves into teams. Dogs often accompanied the huntsmen on the at force hunts. The wild boar was an extremely dangerous animal and would be the main choice of prey for this type of hunt. The teams would chase the prey to near exhaustion or would corner the animal just before the 'kill'.

The bow and stable hunts were the less strenuous forms of hunting. These were designed for less active, or infirm men. This type of hunt was conducted on horseback using a bow as the main weapon.

Dogs also accompanied the hunt and would drive the prey into an enclosed space where the huntsmen could kill the animal at close range. The docile deer would normally be the main choice of prey for this type of hunt.

In 1486, a book called *The Boke of St Albans* was printed – interestingly, it contains the earliest example of colour printing. The book was an old English text on the history of hunting. The author is unknown, but the *Boke of St Albans* is interesting as it details medieval hunting, heraldry and hawking. It provides a list of the animals hunted in medieval England as follows:

The stag – "The stag was usually hunted with aid of dogs and bows and arrows, in order to stay out of range of the horns. Suitable as the prey for 'bow and stable' hunting."

The hart or roebuck – "Usually hunted with aid of dogs and bows and arrows. Suitable as the prey for 'bow and stable' hunting."

Boar – "Usually hunted with the aid of dogs and with very long spears, in order to stay away from the tusks. Suitable as the prey for 'at force' hunting."

The book goes on to list many other quarry species and the type of hunting for which they are suited.

As an example: Foxes – "Usually hunted by chasing them with dogs and letting the dogs tear the fox apart. Foxes are rarely

William I's creation of vast forests for the purpose of hunting shaped the English landscape

Chapter 1: History of Wild Boar in Britain

hunted as food. Suitable as the prey for 'bow and stable' hunting." It also lists rabbits, otters and game birds.

Although not necessarily to do with wild boar, the medieval hunter was adept at using dogs in the pursuit of his quarry. Hunting dogs were bred primarily to work with people to hunt animals, fish and birds. Sight hounds specialised in hunting their quarry by sight, while scent hounds specialised in following the scent or the smell of its quarry. Hunting dogs that relied strongly on the sense of smell to follow the trail of a prey, such as the bloodhound, quite literally follow their noses. As today, types of dog were specifically bred for hunting different prey.

The Tudor dynasty was famous for its advocacy of hunting, with Henry VIII and Elizabeth I being famous for their love of the chase. Sadly it was also this period that saw the end of free ranging wild boar in Britain.

Hunting was viewed as an essential mark of a gentleman and was valued as a test of courage, strength, and agility. It became a main 'pastyme' of the Tudor monarchs, especially Henry VIII. It was said that when he first came to the throne in 1509, finally out from under the strict eye of his father, Henry spent much of his time preoccupied with women and hunting.

He and his many courtiers would often spend a great deal of the day hunting, leaving little time to govern the country. By the 1520s, the number of courtiers hunting with the King had been reduced. Therefore, hunting with the King was an honour, and being invited, or not, was a tell-tale sign of one's real rank in the King's favour.

Hunting was: "A royal and aristocratic sport, almost as prestigious as warfare, and required the same courage and skills as were needed in battle... the quarry, which was usually deer and when possible wild boar, was either shot with bows and arrows, tracked down by dogs, or driven into nets, then ceremoniously killed." (*The King and his Court*, Alison Weir, 2002.)

The deer and wild boars were chased by the King and his company on horseback. The King owned a staggering 200 horses for just such activities. It is likely that by this time the wild boars that were chased were kept on managed private estates purely for the hunt.

Once, while hunting a wild boar, Henry came face to face with death, or at least severe injury, when a wild boar turned on him. Only a quick acting peasant girl who shot the beast down with her bow and arrow saved him.

The meat gained from the sport did not go to waste. Often the meat was given to local peasants, or placed upon the King's own table. It is on record that Henry wrote to Anne Boleyn telling her that he was sending her a large amount of game for her table.

Hunting in Europe with specially bred and trained dogs was the sport of nobles and the clergy, in large part because they owned or controlled much of the land suitable for hunting. Hunting with 'sighthounds' in this era hadn't changed much since the time of Romans. It was a sport, not the serious pursuit of food, which pitted the hounds against the hare and against each other.

Queen Elizabeth I loved to hunt and the event became an auspicious occasion in which the rich nobles were able to show off their fine horses, hawks, clothing, and weapons. Horses were most commonly ranked by endurance, speed, beauty, and strength. Field sports provided not only a hobby, but also a moral means of escape from the rigours of everyday life.

In France, after the hart was killed, the chief huntsman cut off one of its feet and

handed it, on his knees, to the King; in England, the huntsman, also on his knees, handed the hunting knife to the King, who stabbed the hart's carcase as if he were killing the hart.

This English practice was adopted whenever Elizabeth I hunted. The poet George Turberville, who wrote *The Noble Art of Venerie*, stressed the importance of not going through this ritual until the hart was safely dead: "For if the Queen really tried to kill the hart, she might be seriously hurt or even killed, for a hart at bay could inflict great damage on its pursuers".

The hart is a frightened beast, which normally did not dare to look at the weakest man in his kingdom, and this inspired Turberville to some philosophical reflections.

"It should be a warning to princes not to oppress a humble subject and goad him into standing in his own defence, and like the worm, turn again when it is trodden so".

Turberville then hastened to add that his words must not be interpreted as condemning hunting, for that would be contrary to his whole purpose in writing the book.

Hunting was deemed by most to be not only a symbol of knighthood, but an activity that marked out the true gentleman. Those of rank were expected to take part because sporting events trained men for war, whereas the labourers had to work six days a week and could not participate.

The animals that were hunted the most were the stag or buck, and again, where possible – and on the continent, wild boar. When the prey was felled, it was always eaten. During mid-winter, when stag could not be hunted, the Royals and their nobles engaged in hawking.

For Henry VIII, hunting provided him with a chance to escape from the cares of politics with a few friends:

"Pastime with good company
love and shall until I die
Grudge to lust, but none deny
So God be pleased, thus live will I
For my pastance,
Hunt, sing and dance,
My heart is set,
All goodly sport
For my comfort:
Who shall me let"

For others, such as the poet Henry Howard, Earl of Surrey, hunting was associated with a nostalgic, lost happiness. When he was imprisoned in Windsor Castle for striking Edward Seymour, Earl of Hertford, Henry Howard wrote wistfully of how, as a companion to the King's illegitimate son, Henry Fitzroy, Duke of Richmond: "With cry of hounds and merry blasts between, Where we did chase the fearful hart and swine a force."

As an enjoyable recreation, then, hunting provided an essential contrast to a gentleman's daily business, and he had notable and ancient support in this. Pliny, for example, had argued that hunting provided the gentleman with a necessary change from his usual work.

Morally, hunting could be justified as a means of avoiding idleness. Arrogantly, a young Henry VIII announced that: "Hunting was a means to avoid Idlenes the ground of all vyce and to exercise that thing that shalbe honorable and to the bodye healthfull and profitable."

Hunting had been an integral part of a child of the gentry's education since ancient times, and during the 16th century this appears to have remained true.

Although the early part of the 16th century saw a reformation in the style of education that a young noble received, it was still essential that the child had an understanding of the ways of the hunt. According to the mid-15th-century *Boke*

Elizabeth I was a great lover of hunting, and it became an integral part of British life during the period

Chapter 1: HISTORY OF WILD BOAR IN BRITAIN

of Curtesy, which says nothing on how to hunt, it was necessary for the noble child to have knowledge of what money was due to the huntsmen, the bread they were owed, and the number of bones that should be given to each dog. It must therefore have been essential for these children to know how the hunting establishment fitted into the wider organisation of the household. The young gentleman of the late 15th century also had to learn the household etiquette relating to the hunt and in particular to its produce, venison.

Early Tudor huntsmen used a range of specialised weaponry to pursue and kill their prey. For boar, a special spear and sword, or 'tokke', both with cross bars beneath the point designed to prevent boar running up the blade and reaching the huntsmen. Aristocrats such as the Duke of Suffolk and the Marquis of Dorset both used this type of weapon when they were on detachment to the French court.

Lord Montague presented King Henry with a hunting sword, which was described as one with: "The hefte being gilt", at the New Year celebrations of 1532.

Despite this specialisation, weapons were similar enough to be interchangeable and hunting weapons were occasionally used in real fighting. An Irish soldier was stabbed with a boar spear by a German mercenary in 1544 during an affray that followed Henry VIII's capture of Boulogne. Hunting also provided a valuable exercise in shooting. The favoured weapon was the crossbow, and many of the references to this weapon in the armouries of the ruling elite may have been for hunting rather than for war.

In Henry VIII's Hertfordshire palace of Hunsdon in 1539, there were two crossbows, complete with 14 forked arrows, which were clearly designed for the huntsman. There are no surviving references to shooting with the gun, which was beginning to make archery a redundant skill on the battlefield. The gun was perhaps too inaccurate at this stage to make much impact on the hunting field, although Henry VIII did have a specially made breach loader.

The animal hunted was ordinarily the stag, which in the Tudor period was usually called the hart. Although the English wild swine was not considered as fierce or fleet of foot as the boar in Europe, it was still a worthy opponent in the royal parks.

Sometimes a buck was hunted instead of a hart. Yeomen farmers hunted foxes, but no gentleman did until the end of the 17th century.

When a hart or buck was killed, it was eaten. Harts could be hunted at most times of the year, but not in mid-winter, and the King and his nobles then engaged in hawking instead. Falcons were trained for this sport, and statutes were passed to punish any poacher who stole their eggs.

The pursuit of animals on horseback or on foot, more than other types of hunting,

Henry VIII was a passionate hunter who nearly suffered injury at the hands of a cornered wild boar

was important because it provided good exercise, or 'valiaunt motion of the spirites' by which 'all thinges superfluous be expelled, and the conduits of the body clensed'. Riding at speed gave the hunter such exercise, while he was necessarily out in fresh air, which, according to the early Tudor physician Andrew Boorde was an essential element in healthy living. Hunting was valuable not only for its health benefits, but because it was a means of exercising the gentleman's manliness or prowess.

Henry VIII took King William's forest laws a step further and made unauthorised hunting in private forests a felony punishable by death if the offence was committed at night, but during the daylight hours it was only a trespass punishable by fine or imprisonment.

Commoners who hunted with greyhounds in defiance of these laws favoured dogs whose colouring made them harder to spot: black, red, fawn, and brindle.

Nobles by contrast favoured white and spotted dogs that could be spotted and recovered more easily if lost in the forest. It became common among the English aristocracy to say: "You could tell a gentleman by his horses and his greyhounds."

King James I certainly preferred hunting to hard work. He was an avid fan of greyhound coursing. Having heard about the strength of the local hares, he brought his greyhounds to the village of Fordham near the border of Suffolk and Cambridge.

This was a private competition between the King's greyhounds and was observed by James and his court. He enjoyed the coursing in Suffolk so much that he built a hunting lodge in the area and to improve the quality of hunting, in 1619 he ordered that the release of hares and partridges should take place every year at Newmarket. James I must have been an early conservationist because it would seem that he had also tried re-introducing wild boar in to Windsor park in 1608, but ultimately the attempt would appear to have been unsuccessful.

Races between the horses of his followers became as popular as the matches between the King's greyhounds, and this began the tradition of competitive racing in Suffolk.

Hunting gifts were frequently given in order to ensure lasting friendships between attendees. The Lisle family, whose letters provide us with the most complete view of a noble family's gift-giving activities, showed that they gave venison and wild boar to not only friends and relations, but also to a wide variety of people, from the King downwards.

Arthur Plantagenet, Lord Lisle, sent a large number of small wild birds to Henry VIII in July 1535, which apparently kept Henry 'merry' in Epping Forest that summer.

Thomas Cranmer sent a buck and a wild boar to the master of Jesus College, Cambridge, as part of his good will as the newly appointed Archbishop of Canterbury. Other important nobles displayed their charitable nature to the poorer members of the community by adding to their special communal meals venison and wild boar, or returning favours from their local communities with similar gifts.

By the close of the 16th century, the world had changed significantly. Feudalism had ended, allowing commoners freedom of movement unknown for a thousand years. City dwellers increased in number. By this time many more people were able to own game dogs such as greyhounds. As the number of middle class persons expanded, so did the need for cleared land. Dense forests and swamps were giving way to planting land, pastures, and towns. These

Chapter 1 HISTORY OF WILD BOAR IN BRITAIN

new fields brought infiltration by hares, foxes, and badgers.

Wild boar – an increasing nuisance to pig breeders a century before – had ceased to be a problem because, due to deforestation and excessive hunting, they simply no longer existed. Since the start of the 15th century, pig farmers went from constantly having their pens broken into and their domestic sows covered by rampaging boar excited by the smell of females in oestrus, to being totally wild boar free. The need to exterminate unwanted animals and the Tudors love of hunting led to, among other things, the end of wild boar in Britain.

EXTINCTION IN BRITAIN

It is difficult to put a date on when wild boar actually ceased to roam freely in Britain because throughout history there have been attempts to re-introduce them. It is likely however that most of the boar that Henry VIII hunted here would have been animals that had been brought over from France and put into royal parks and forests. Truly free ranging wild boar, ones that had their ancestral line originating from this country, may have become extinct in Great Britain as early as the 13th century. After this date they were kept for game and status in private parks, after importing them in from France and Germany. There seems to have been a number of attempts at re-introduction between the 13th and 17th centuries; as already mentioned, we know that James I of England (VI of Scotland) tried this twice in Windsor Park. The main reason for their demise seems to have been largely because of widespread deforestation, especially during the reign of Elizabeth I, and intensive hunting.

Between the 17th century and the 1980s there were no wild boar, native or introduced, in Britain apart from a handful that may have been kept as exhibits in zoos.

FARMING WILD BOAR IN THE UK

The commercial farming of wild boar started in the 1980s, which may have come about due to the economic boom of that period. People were tending to travel more, and with that they may have developed a more cosmopolitan palate. Wild boar, after all, had been on the menu of continental restaurants for many years. Following the demand for wild boar in British butchers and restaurants, a few entrepreneurial English farmers imported the first wild boar to come to these shores for 300 years.

They are listed under the Dangerous Wild Animals Act 1976, which requires keepers to be licensed. I have kept wild boar for the best part of 20 years and as well as being controlled by the department of environmental health, my animals also have a veterinary inspection annually. They are kept in large enclosures that are behind a high fence with three strands of barbed wire along the top and a snout wire along the ground. As if all that is not enough, the enclosure is also protected with an electric fence.

The idiocy of needing them to be licensed is something that I have never understood, and here is the reason.

I also keep a few rare breed pigs, some of which are, from time to time crossed with wild boar. I do this in order to produce what are sometimes called 'Iron Age' pigs, which make excellent eating. Domestic pigs can be kept, of course, without the need of a DWA licence, and yet over the years I have never had a wild boar that was too dangerous to handle, but I have had several very nasty domestic boars, especially Tamworths. Apart from that, the damage caused by an escapee, or the risk of infection caused by a diseased animal, is exactly the same whether the porcine is wild or domestic.

Because of the peripatetic lifestyle of wild boar the meat is usually very lean

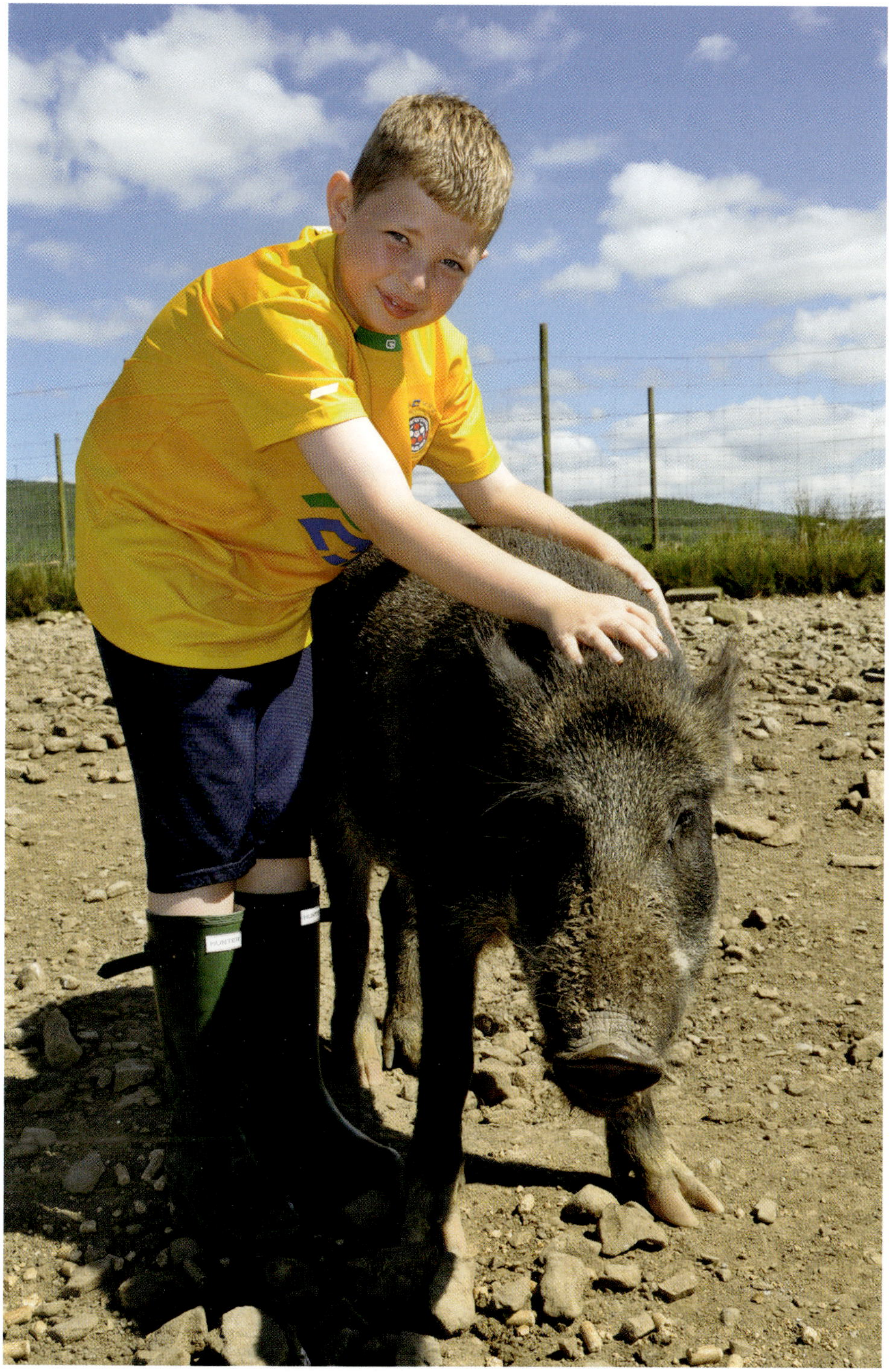

The commercial farming of wild boar took off in the UK during the economic boom of the 1980s

Chapter 1 HISTORY OF WILD BOAR IN BRITAIN

and unlike pig meat is red, more like beef in appearance. In its natural habitat the animal will eat a great variety of food, which will lead to the meat developing a range of flavours far fuller than any domestic beast. Dependent on age, it can taste gamey at one end of the spectrum, to equivalent to the best cut of beef that you have ever tasted at the other.

In 2000 two seemingly entrepreneurial Scottish farmers applied to the Scottish Office for a grant to do a feasibility study on the merits of farming wild boar under the Marketing Development Scheme that SEERAD (Scottish Executive Environment and Rural Affairs Department) was running at that time. Allegedly the grant was paid, but that was the last that was heard of The Scottish Farmed Wild Boar Association as I believe it was to be called.

By this time an enterprising farmer from Perthshire named Andrew Johnston had been experimenting with wild boar for some time as a part of a farm diversification scheme. After seeing the success that some wild boar farmers were enjoying in England, Andrew purchased 10 wild boars from a breeder in Essex and so the successful Hilton Wild Boar Farm was born.

Andrew had a number of years rearing and selling wild boar meat to farmers' markets, farm shops and retailing through his own butcher's shop. At the height of production he had as many as 100 breeding sows.

Nowadays wild boar production is more of a sideline to his mainstream farming business, and this was brought about largely because of the difficulty in getting abattoirs to slaughter these animals.

In the early days he used an abattoir in Dunblane, but the cost became prohibitive because of the introduction of testing for *Trichinella spiralis* or pork worm, so he took his business to a slaughterhouse in St Andrews where he was able to secure a better deal. In July 2013 the St Andrews establishment closed its doors for the last time and Andrew re-negotiated terms at Dunblane once again, albeit this time with a much smaller throughput in mind.

Ironically testing for the nematode *Trichinella* is arguably a redundant measure as there has not been an incident of infection in commercial pig herds in Europe for many years. The prevalence is estimated to be less than one in 100,000. However it is believed that the incidence may be higher in free ranging wild boar (not farm reared) from some parts of Europe.

A result of the 2004 Agricultural Census showed that at the time there were around 100 holdings with around 2,800 breeding sows, including domestic pig/boar hybrids in England. Farmed herd sizes ranged from less than 10 to over 130 breeding sows. Meat from these farms is subject to the same hygiene standards as domestic pigs.

In 2004 approximately 1,500,000 tons of domestic pig meat was consumed and there were about five million pigs in the UK. In the same year the wild boar market was estimated to be 500,000kg in weight and worth £2million.

RETURN TO THE WILD

Since the pig farming boom in the 1980s, there have been a number of escapes that have led to several feral populations becoming established throughout the UK.

According to DEFRA, in a study carried out by Wilson et al in 2006, there are three significant populations that have established themselves in England.

The largest group that was studied at that time was in Kent/East Sussex and it was estimated that there were approximately 200 animals. Another group in West Dorset

was estimated at being fewer than 50 animals, while the population in the third area of the Wye Valley/Forest of Dean appeared to fluctuate between fewer than 30 to more than 50 animals. The reason for the fluctuation was thought to be due to a hard cull followed by compensatory reproduction.

In my opinion it is about as difficult to estimate the number of wild boar on a home range as it is to estimate the number of roe deer in a given area. Most informed opinions, I believe, would agree that it is a challenging task to perform – unless you have at your disposal military aircraft with sophisticated search equipment on board. One difficult arises from the fact that it is rather similar to quantum physics where the act of observation will influence the outcome.

The Mammal Society says: "Article 11 of the Bern Convention (European Union 1982) requires member states 'to encourage the reintroduction of native species of wild flora and fauna when this would contribute to the conservation of an endangered species.' It is unlikely that wild boar falls under this article, as it is not an endangered species in Europe; indeed it is regarded as a pest in many agricultural areas. However, as a native species The Mammal Society would, in principle, like to see wild boar re-established in this country."

As the reader will no doubt learn, I totally concur with the Mammal Society and believe that it is about time that the wild boar was recognised as being an indigenous species and given a legitimate status as a game animal.

Chapter 1 — HISTORY OF WILD BOAR IN BRITAIN

Although I am a strong advocate of allowing wild boar to re-establish themselves as an indigenous species, I do of course realise that if this were to happen it may have implications that need to be thought out carefully and control measures put in place. It has been at least 300 years since wild boars have inhabited our countryside and many things, not least of which the human population itself, have changed in that time. The impact of re-introduction may therefore have uncertain repercussions. Unlike in America where the state owns the wildlife, in the UK wild animals belong to no one, and it is unclear whether the presence of a potentially dangerous wild animal on land might render landowners liable in some circumstances.

There are many concerns with the concept of allowing wild boars to roam free in the countryside in the 21st century. One realistic opinion is that because of the low age at which wild boars are able to reproduce, the species would become widespread relatively quickly. Added to this they have relatively large litters and no natural predators in Britain. Clearly some form of control would need to be put in place to address these issues, quite likely in some areas more than others. Certainly if these populations are allowed to develop, legislation must be revised to formalise the legal requirements covering use of firearms. This would mean the insistence of a minimum calibre as well as well-defined shooting seasons; all this of course would require new legislation to be put in place.

DEFRA carried out two risk assessments in 2007, one was concerned with the spread of disease in livestock and the other was on risks to biodiversity, agricultural damage and human health and safety. Again I believe that the authorities are perfectly correct in assessing the potential risks involved in allowing a re-introduced animal to roam unchecked.

The findings of the report were in fact that the risk was actually very low, which then gives support to the many people like me who would welcome a return of these magnificent animals to the British Isles.

DEFRA'S POSITION

In their policy paper Feral Wild Boar in England – An Action Plan, DEFRA set out to explain where they stood on the question of the management of wild boar in the country. The plan, a 56-page document, details what the department's position is based on risk assessments.

In summary, DEFRA's underlying strategy for managing wildlife starts from the position of no intervention, unless it becomes necessary on the basis of sound evidence. In the case of conflicting priorities they aim to ensure the most appropriate outcome.

Further to this, and on the basis of the risk assessments mentioned previously, as well as taking into account the number of wild boar in a given area at any one time, DEFRA considers that regional management would be the most appropriate approach. In a nutshell, and I quote: "DEFRA's policy is that primary responsibility for feral wild boar management lies with local communities and individual landowners. However, Government will help facilitate this regional management through the provision of advice and guidance."

This way it leaves wide open the option to step in if there is any money to be made or a tax to be collected. Maybe this is déjà vu, but I feel as though I am back at the Battle of Hastings. It would seem that things have not progressed very much since the draconian measures imposed upon us when William the Conqueror took over.

In Scotland they may still be sitting on the fence, but to give the officials the benefit of doubt they are not letting too much out of the bag.

The Scottish government has its own Department for the Environment, Food and Rural Affairs and at the time of this book going to press, John Gray of the Species Management Team talked to me about his department's involvement with wild boar. He admitted that they were not armed with too much evidence on the status quo right now and in the absence of hard facts their policy is much the same as it is in England.

He was aware of anecdotes about wild boar in the Highlands, in the Central belt and in Dumfries and Galloway, but was vague on numbers. I suggested that it sounded as though the Scottish government did not really have a policy. From what I could understand, the status of wild boar north of the border was that of vermin. He agreed, indicating that that was pretty much the case. However Mr Gray did say: "Before a management policy could be worked on, the department was waiting for a study to be carried out by Scottish National Heritage," which apparently is in the pipeline.

THE BIOLOGY OF WILD BOAR

The term wild boar is slightly misleading in so much as the word boar is generally the name given to an adult male of several animal species, including the domestic pig. In this case, however, it refers to the whole species, and as such there are wild boar boars as well as wild boar sows.

Wild boar (*Sus scrofa*) are also commonly known as wild pigs, razorbacks and wild hogs, and may be found all over Europe, Asia and North Africa. The species found in the UK are known as Eurasian wild boar, although this is an over simplification in terms of taxonomy, and are most likely to be of the sub species *Sus scrofa scrofa* or European wild boar. This sub species is indigenous to most of the north-western European countries, such as France, Germany, Belgium, some parts of Scandanavia, western Poland and Czechoslovakia, although it should be said that unlike the French, for example, we do not have extensive genetic data on our wild boar here in the UK and so their precise origin is somewhat indeterminate.

To some extent DNA sampling is arbitrary because there has never been a standard by which to measure purity. Due to historical hybridisation between wild boar and domestic pigs or wild boar of different sub species, DNA testing will only reveal a difference between one individual and another with no indication of what is a pure bred animal.

The French, who take the problem of purity very seriously, use chromosome numbers as an indication of the integrity of the blood line. They know that their wild boar have 36 chromosomes while domestic pigs have 38. A hybrid wild boar domestic pig cross has 37, and therefore a beast that looks like a wild boar but does not have 36 chromosomes is by definition not a true wild boar.

This does not seem to work outside of France, however, and in some parts of mainland Europe wild boar also have 38 chromosomes. There is also evidence of spontaneous occurrences of wild boar having 37 or 38 chromosomes being found in all areas.

APPEARANCE

The wild boar is a thick set, powerful animal covered in coarse, dense, bristly hair that varies in colour from black to light grey tinged with light brown. It carries the bulk of its weight at the front end where the large, triangular shaped head is supported by massive shoulders with no apparent neck.

The body then tapers off to lower, more slender hind quarters, sporting a straight tail with long tufts of hair at the end. Body length in the male is about 1.5m, with the female being slightly shorter. The legs are stout and quite muscular and are of a length commensurate with the rest of the animal's size, which makes a good male stand at about 90cm at the shoulder.

The foot of *Sus scrofa* has four toes, but only the middle two are used to support

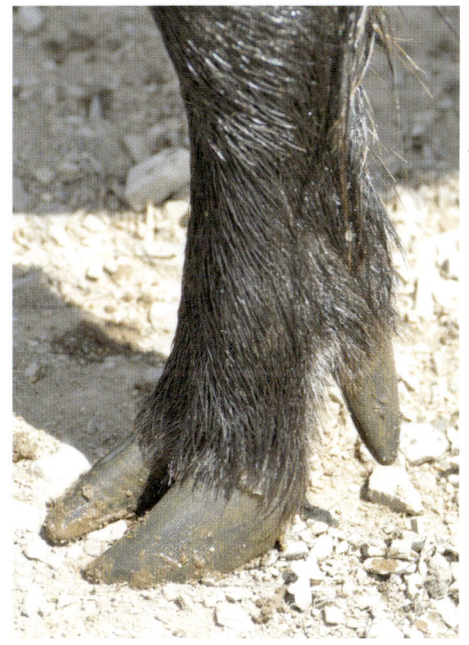

the body, while the two lateral toes or false hoof are higher up and do not generally touch the ground.

The wild boar has a powerful, long tapering snout that ends in a cartilaginous disc, which it uses for digging and searching for food. Its sense of smell is extremely well developed, certainly on a par with most dogs, and is responsible not only for self-defence but also for finding food, which it does by sniffing the ground for buried morsels as it journeys around its territory. The olfactory sense is also important not only for marking out boundaries, but also for social recognition, which it does with scented glandular secretions, allowing communication among members of the herd.

The wild boar has very sharp hearing, which is affected by large, non rotational

Above: The boar carries the majority of its weight over powerful front shoulders

Left: Note the false hoof, which generally will not touch the ground

WILD BOAR – A BRITISH PERSPECTIVE

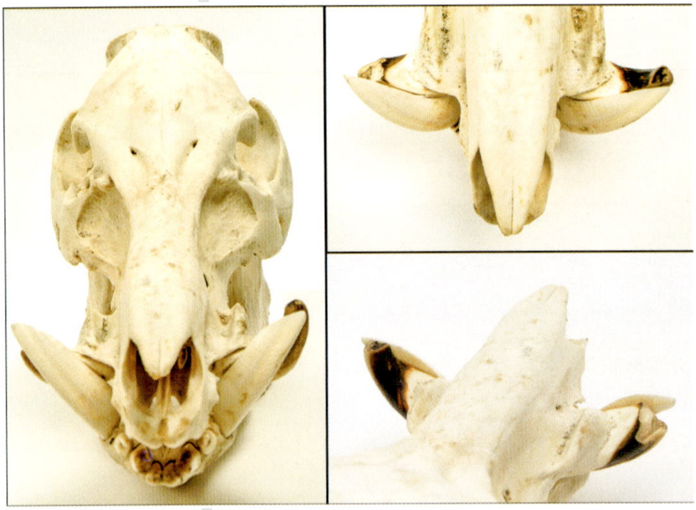

Chapter 2 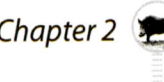 THE BIOLOGY OF WILD BOAR

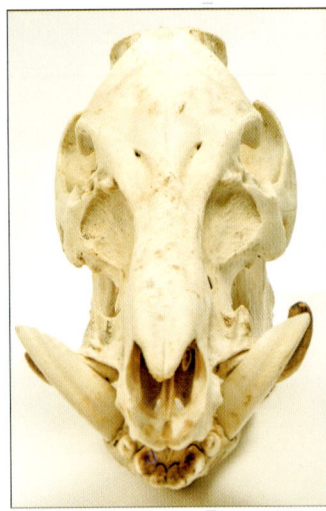

A

B

C

D

Note how the boar's neck slopes forward in A, while the pig's profile is markedly different in B. A wild boar's tail will always be straight with a tassel of long hair at the end, as in C, rather than curled like in image D

ears situated on top of its head. In order to facilitate hearing from all directions the animal has to turn its head or even its whole body.

Visual acuity on the other hand is most definitely not one of the wild boar's greatest assets and is the least developed of all its senses, only really having any effective sight at close quarters. Although the small eyes are incapable of producing a clear image at a distance, they are very good at detecting movement from far away, and this ability will alert the individual to any potential danger. Vision, as with many mammals, is in black and white, the eyes having no colour receptors.

Generally speaking an adult male wild boar will weigh between 60 and 180kg, although occasionally they get much bigger; weights in excess of 300kg have been recorded.

Although quite clearly of the *Suidae* family, wild boar differ from domestic pigs in appearance in a number of ways. These differences are important when considering whether an individual is, on observation, a wild boar or a hybrid. Pure wild boar will have:

36 WILD BOAR – A BRITISH PERSPECTIVE

- A long straight snout with a dark muzzle and straight profile.
- Erect, rigid ears edged with long hair.
- Heavy large shoulders that slope down to much lighter hind quarters.
- The entire body is covered in a thick coat of hair for most of the year.
- Piglets are born with horizontal stripes.
- The tail is always straight ending in a tassel of long hair.
- The tail is held high when the individual is alarmed.

On the other hand, domestic pigs and hybrids will have:
- A much broader head with a shorter snout that has a concave profile.
- Ears that are often broader and less rigid. They are sometimes quite floppy in the style of a domestic Large Black pig whose ears cover the eyes.
- Tail always has a twist.
- The shoulders and hind quarters are far more uniform in size.
- Skin and hooves often splashed with pink.

These differences are not always very pronounced especially if the domestic influence in the bloodline is from several generations back, but on close inspection one or more of these differences will be apparent.

BEHAVIOUR

In most senses of the word, wild boar are gregarious, living in small family units known as sounders, which are more commonly called herds. These family cells will even tolerate each other at wallows or watering holes, mixing together and then going about their business as separate entities. However the mature males are far more solitary, only coming into contact with the sounders when a female comes into oestrus.

In fact the social organisation of these animals is quite complicated and actually covers a community life that comprises a broad spectrum of behaviour that can range between the two extremes described above.

The sounder will be led by a mature sow and will consist of several adult females that may or may not be pregnant or suckling youngsters. The sounder may also include last year's youngsters, both male and female, from females in the group.

When young boars reach adulthood at around 15 months old they will be eased out of the matriarchal unit and will be forced to form a group of sub-adult males; a situation that is often precipitated by the arrival of a dominant boar coming into the group at the time of the rut.

As well as the difference in the snouts of pure wild boar and pigs, the boar's ears, shown in E, stand erect, while a hybrid or pig's ears are floppy

WILD BOAR – A BRITISH PERSPECTIVE

Sub-adult females may also join the juvenile bachelor herd as a result of the break-up of a maternal herd; often because of the loss of the dominant sow. This loss may be due to natural causes or quite often because of uncontrolled or irresponsible hunting.

TERRITORIES

The home ranges of wild boar vary considerably in size and are usually defined not only by physical size, but also by the period of time spent in them. The range or territory will therefore include all places that the individual visits within that time span. Within that large area, which may also be visited by wild boar from other sounders or groups, will be a smaller territory that is guarded and considered off limits to outsiders. Annual home ranges of 120-150km^2 for males and 40-60km^2 for females have been recorded in some European countries, but it's more common to see average seasonal or monthly home ranges from 1.1km^2 to over 50km^2.

In the UK, radio-tracking of 18 sub-adult animals by Central Science Laboratory (CSL) in 2004 in the Weald and Ross-on-Wye areas gave range sizes of 1.0-9.6km^2 for animals tracked for between one and 12 months.

As individuals leave their parent sounders and look for their own territories they move further and further from their place of origin. Long distance dispersal movements of up to 300km for males and 100km for females have been reported, and even large rivers present little obstacle to dispersal. However, normal dispersal distances tend to be far smaller, and in England the maximum distance recorded by a radio-tracked animal was a male who moved 20km from the site where he was trapped.

Territories expand as the population density becomes too much for a particular area, and this of course will depend on factors such as availability of food, pressure from hunting, and proximity to human disturbance. Therefore population densities for boar vary widely; typical numbers in continental Europe range from two to five per km^2.

Understanding the dynamics of wild boar territories is important in their management because, due to their large ranges, it is quite likely that they will be hunted by more than one group or syndicate of shooters. Clearly this becomes a problem if one hunter kills the product of another hunter's careful management. Sadly, however, in the UK most wild boar are more likely to be considered vermin than legitimate game animals and therefore they tend to be randomly shot rather than being a part of a management programme. This, I believe, is a situation that should not be tolerated, and our wildlife agencies and conservation organisations should be lobbied to introduce hunting seasons and more specific protection by law.

REPRODUCTION

The social structure of wild boar is based on related females living in groups or sounders, along with sub-adults and juveniles. Mature males lead a largely solitary existence for most of the year, but will join the female groups for the rut, which is at its height between November and January. It should be explained that the rut is not quite the same in wild boar as it is in, for example, deer. A hind will come in to season just once a year, largely in October, with calves being born mostly during May and June. A sow on the other hand can come into oestrus every 21 days, which means that potentially she could be covered by the boar at any time of the year. However there are a lot of environmental factors that can affect the sow coming into heat, such as feeding conditions, peer pressure within the hierarchy of the sounder, and human disturbance, including hunting.

The timing of the rut seems to be dictated more by the boars who reach their annual peak of condition by November and determinedly seek out females that are in season. Sexual activity and testosterone production in males is triggered by decreasing day length, which reaches a peak in mid-autumn. This also gives the sows and their youngsters an advantage by farrowing when the worst of the winter weather is past. The gestation period for a sow is the same as it is for domestic pigs: three months, three weeks and three days. During this time, and while she is suckling her squeakers, the sow will not come back into oestrus. Her season is also affected by a phenomenon known as photoperiodism, which means that a female's season is affected by the length of daylight hours. During the long days of the summer months she will not come into oestrus. Once autumn comes, the abundance of food initiates the cycle and her seasons start up again.

It is normally the older females in the group that come into heat first and their role is of great importance as they will mark their home range with secretions

Top: Sexual activity among boar reaches its peak in November

Left: A painting by Elizabeth Halstead, which was commissioned by the author, of two male boar clashing over a female

WILD BOAR – A BRITISH PERSPECTIVE

Chapter 2 — THE BIOLOGY OF WILD BOAR

from lachrymal glands near the eyes, signalling that they are ready for mating. Younger sows then copy this behaviour as they to come into season.

As a solitary boar moves into the sow's territory he will then mark his journey with copious amounts of froth from his mouth, which gives him the appearance of a rabid dog. He will also mark his tracks with urine with the intention of dissuading other boar from moving in on his females.

When two boars do meet on these occasions it is likely that a battle will commence, although it is generally quite short lived.

I once commissioned an oil painting by the wildlife artist Elizabeth Halstead of just such an encounter that I had photographed in south-west Scotland.

The skirmish normally starts with the combatants coming shoulder to shoulder, preparing to do each other harm with their formidable tusks. A lot of snorting follows in an attempt to discourage each other, but usually one will back off before any real harm is done. Even so, some of these clashes can look pretty spectacular with the most dominant boar gaining victory and therefore the favour of the females. Mating can last over 45 minutes, and involves much chasing around, with the boar finally mounting the sow. Afterwards the boar rolls over and goes to sleep – nothing new there then!

Actually that is not quite true, he is more likely to wander off sniffing the rest of the sounder to determine whether another sow is receptive, in which case the whole process is repeated.

The sow will prepare for farrowing by finding a suitable spot to make a nest. This is usually somewhere that she is unlikely to be disturbed and that is sheltered from inclement weather. I have actually seen inexperienced young females and sows that have been bullied and cast from the sounder make nests out in the open, completely exposed to the elements.

When first born, the piglets or, as I like to call them, humbugs, have horizontal stripes, hence the name, and weigh between 1.8-2.2lbs. If the nest is well placed and lined with dry leaves and other materials, the humbugs will stay there for up to 10 days, with the mother leaving them only briefly to feed. At this time she will be very protective and not allow anyone to approach.

Generally wild boar will only have one litter per year, but occasionally, during very favourable conditions, a sow may have two. Their litters are usually smaller than with the domestic pig, and a younger wild boar will have a smaller litter than a more mature animal. A small young female is likely to produce between one and five squeakers, while a larger, heavier sow will give birth to between three and seven. Most farrowing then takes place between March and May as a result of a November to January rut.

The sex ratio of the squeakers across the board is 1:1, although that is not to say that an individual litter may not have more males than females, or vice versa.

A newborn piglet or wild boarlet will be up on its feet very quickly with eyes open and will be fully able to totter around unaided. The squeaker detaches itself from the umbilicus without assistance from its mother and will fight its siblings to get to its mother's teat with determination and aggression right from the beginning.

A pecking order develops very quickly and within just a few days each humbug has its own teat from which to feed. If necessary the litter are able to follow the sow in order to escape danger. After a week the litter will be foraging on the floor for food, although at this stage they will not actually be eating it. From about two weeks they begin to absorb solid food, then at about two months they are weaned off milk and are able to eat a diet similar to that of the adult.

During this time the sow will have rejoined the sounder or aligned herself with other young females to start a new family unit. By the time the squeakers are six months old they will all but have lost their stripes and begin to take on their winter moult.

The females of the litter will then reach puberty any time from eight to 24 months of age, largely depending upon when they were born. Becoming pubescent is closely aligned with body weight and general condition; a well-nourished adolescent will reach puberty sooner than a youngster that was born during a period of food shortage. The female will generally be around 70lbs by the time she is ready to conceive.

Wild boar can live up to 10 years in the wild, but where they are heavily hunted there are likely to be very few animals more than five or six years old.

The young boarlets, or humbugs due to their horizontal stripes, follow their mother to avoid danger. By two months they will have been weaned off milk

WILD BOAR – A BRITISH PERSPECTIVE 41

Chapter 2 — THE BIOLOGY OF WILD BOAR

Boar have an affinity to water, which extends to squeezing into drinking troughs to bathe and cool down

HABITAT AND FEEDING

Wild boars show a remarkable ability to adapt to almost any type of habitat in the temperate zone, although they have a preference for deciduous woodland or other habitats that provide suitable cover. They will happily colonise arable ground as well as forests, sometimes causing massive destruction to crops such as maize, where they are able to shelter as well as feed. They will adapt to mountainous regions as well as low lying marshland. Wild boars have a real love of water, which they will not hesitate to enter if being chased or for pure enjoyment, especially in hot weather. I have often watched in amusement as many as three sows trying to fit into a water trough, not to drink, but simply to bathe or cool down. Another reason for liking the water is that the wild boar has an enormous appetite for fish, whether it is the dead fish that anglers have left behind on the banks of a river or the more abundant resources of commercial fish farms.

A wild boar is usually content if it has got food, water and plenty of cover. Being in an undisturbed environment is especially important during daytime and sows are particularly associated with making use of dense cover. Open habitats are used mainly at night time, for feeding and travelling between different parts of the home range.

Deciduous forests not only provide good cover, but also a diverse array of food, ranging from roots, acorns, and beech masts, to fungi and fruits, such as crab apples and blackberries. That is quite apart from the multitude of insects, grubs and larvae, small reptiles and amphibians, such as lizards and frogs, and small mammals, for example mice and voles, they eat.

Coniferous forests on the other hand, while providing a degree of cover, tend to be more sterile beneath their canopy, with food being far less in abundance.

Another habitat favoured by wild boar is open farmland that is criss crossed with thick hedgerows and which has small coppiced plantations. Although they tend not to stay in this type of area for too long, while they are present they can do a lot of damage to cereal or root crops.

Although wild boar are without a doubt opportunistic omnivores, they really will eat almost anything, and around 90 per cent of their diet is made up of a wide variety of vegetable matter. Stalks, roots, acorns, beech nuts, grasses and flowers are particularly prominent components of their dietary intake.

Animal food, such as the examples mentioned above, will only make about 10 per cent of their diet, but will be consumed frequently. Other species taken may include earthworms and snails, while carrion will not be ignored and will be consumed opportunistically.

Where wild boar make themselves public enemy number one is when they take to raiding cultivated plants, and these can make up a large proportion of their diet. Preferred plants include potatoes, beet, maize and other cereals. On the continent deliberate supplementary feeding, often with maize, is important during winter in order to maintain sporting stock numbers.

DENTITION

It is probably wrong to assume that an accurate estimate of age can be deduced from teeth or tusks beyond three years old. Up until that age the jaw continues to develop until a full set of teeth have

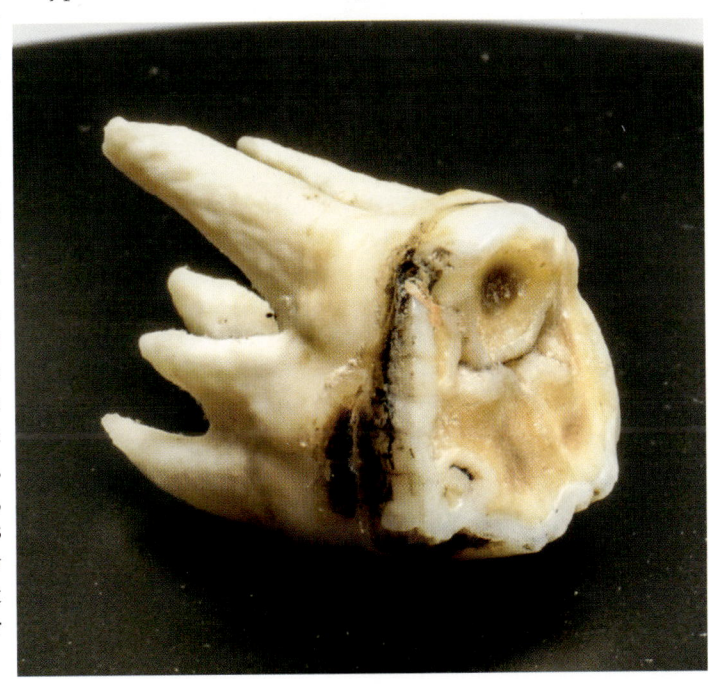

A badly worn molar from a mature boar

WILD BOAR – A BRITISH PERSPECTIVE

Chapter 2 — THE BIOLOGY OF WILD BOAR

Note the sharp edge on these tusks taken from a six-year-old

grown. Beyond three years the molars particularly show signs of wear, the amount of which to some extent depends on the individual's diet throughout its life. Clearly, the more the molars and pre-molars are worn, the more mature the pig is likely to be. The picture on the previous page shows a tooth that has come from an old boar that I know to have been at least eight years old. It looks likely that this would have caused its owner a degree of pain.

Canine tusks grow in both the male and the female, but it is only in male that they grow to an impressive size. The under tusk in the lower jaw grinds and wears away against the smaller upper tusk creating a razor sharp edge. In combat the sow tends to bite, but the boar will raise his head sharply against his opponent slitting open his adversaries legs or flank.

Only one third of the tusk is visible out of the jaw, which protrudes out of the mouth to serve to all a warning that this beast is not to be messed with. A boar that has lost one tusk is known as a mire.

Wild boar have a total of 44 teeth in both jaws, and it is the lower jaw that has the big canines: each half jaw has three incisors, one canine, four pre-molars, and three molars.

WILD BOAR – A BRITISH PERSPECTIVE

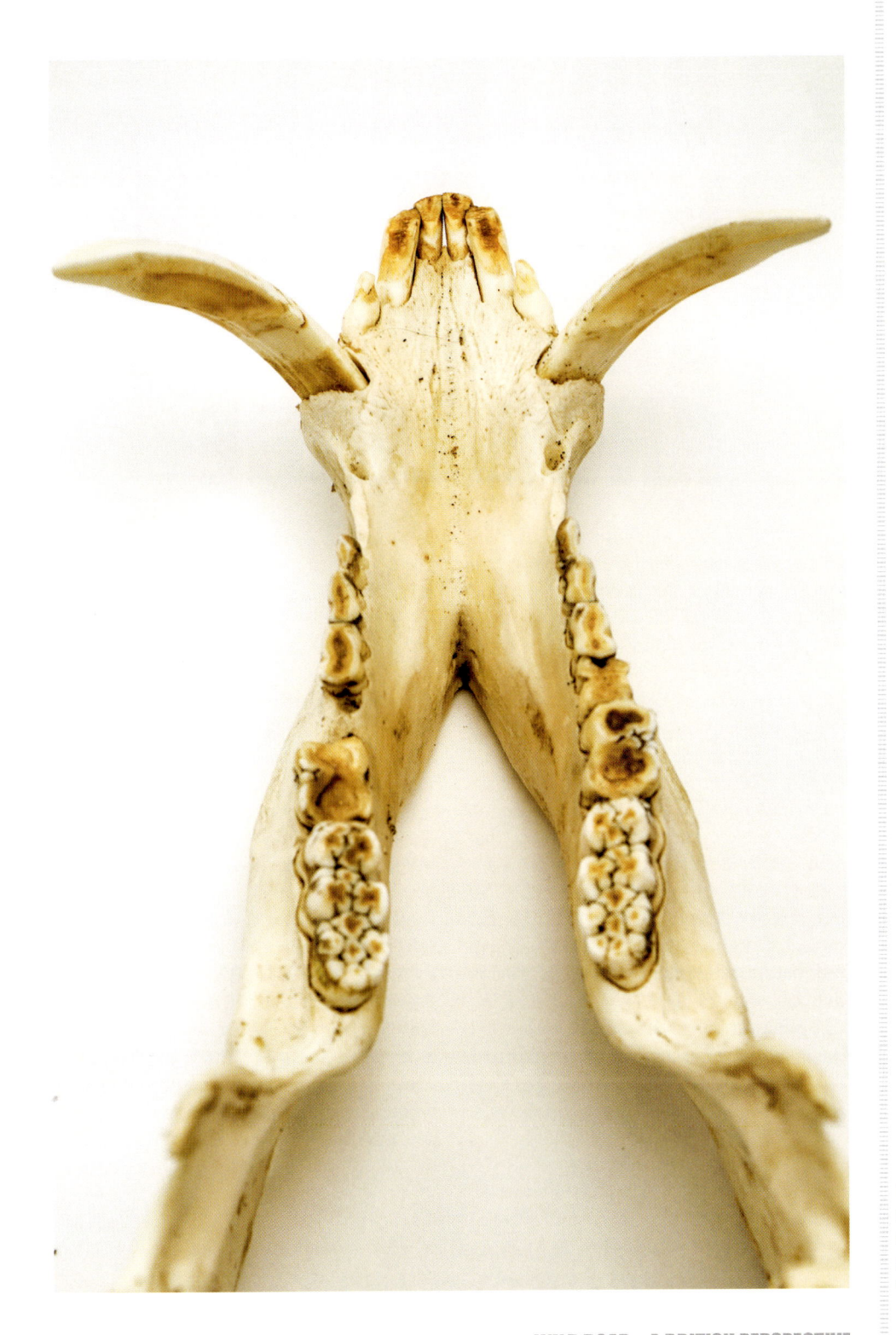

This lower jaw, showing the large canine tusks, has one pre-molar missing on the left side

WILD BOAR – A BRITISH PERSPECTIVE

HUNTING WILD BOAR IN BRITAIN: THE KNOWLEDGE

I began my involvement with wild boar over 30 years ago when a farmer offered me some much sought after deer stalking on his land, but only if I were able to rid him of whatever was causing vast amounts of damage to his maize and root crop.

Every day, he explained with righteous indignation, he would walk out on his fields and find that: "Some beast or other has been digging up my crops and robbing me blind."

He had no idea what was causing all of this damage and, to be honest, at that time neither did I. I didn't let on as much, however, and led him to believe that I had seen this sort of thing before. I told him that I was just the man to sort out his problem and that he would not regret leaving me in charge of security.

I went away from that meeting elated that I had now got an ideal place for roe, muntjac and occasional red stalking, but perplexed as to what was causing the damage to the farmer's property and how I was going to go about rectifying the problem.

To add to my difficulties, the location of the farm was many miles from where I lived. Although it was not too far to go for some recreational stalking at weekends, I felt that in order to resolve this issue I was going to have to spend more than just an hour or two each week finding the cause of this menace, let alone actually dealing with it. I decided to spend a week living in a local B&B and going out on regular day and night time recces in order to first of all find who or what was the culprit, and then hopefully put a stop to this unwanted activity.

Before beginning my campaign I did some rudimentary research, which included asking fellow stalkers and one or two gamekeepers for their opinions; these varied from rampaging badgers to what seemed the most likely explanation: escapees from a local pig farm. It must be remembered that back in the 1970s free ranging wild boar were thought of as a continental, or you might even say exotic, species and not something that you would expect to find roaming the English countryside. They were not unheard of in the UK, but certainly not something that one might expect to encounter when taking the dog for a walk, or indeed to find when out inspecting one's crop of sugar beet or sweetcorn.

Somehow domestic pigs and wayward badgers didn't seem to fit the bill, and so there was nothing for it but to get out there and have a look for myself. Armed with nothing more than a pair of modest binoculars and some warm stalking wear, I spent the next three or four days and nights patrolling the 500 acres of farmland where the marauders had caused their damage. I went out at various times of the day and night, with each foray lasting maybe a couple of hours. Sometimes I would creep around on foot and sometimes, especially at night, I would sit in my Land Rover at some secluded location on the farm and just wait.

After several days I had seen nothing suspicious. A number of roe deer and muntjac had been counted, as well as foxes, a barn owl or two, and even a badger, albeit

UK farmers, gamekeepers and hunters considered free ranging wild boar a continental species during the 1970s

WILD BOAR – A BRITISH PERSPECTIVE

a well behaved one. Nothing even came close to looking like the culprit that I was after and, possibly even worse, there was no fresh evidence of vandalism or pillaging.

Towards the end of my planned week of vigilance word got back to me that there had been similar damage reported on a farm several miles away. I considered going along to ask if I could have a look at the crime scene, but decided that I would simply be spreading myself too thin, and instead braced myself for another long night in the vehicle, as well as foot-patrolling the edge of woods and hedgerows that were in abundance on the property. On that last night I was set to stay out from dusk till dawn, so at least when I reported back to the farmer I could say hand on heart that I tried my best to find the mystery beast.

It was at about 3.00am when something aroused me from the fitful nap I am ashamed to say I was having. A quarter moon had risen well above the horizon and, with an almost cloudless sky, a silvery glow enabled me to scan the knee-high vegetation that was stretching out before me.

Suddenly there it was. Moving among the shadows of the broad leafed sugar beet was a dark mass, clearly some kind of animal and seemingly foraging with its head down. As I looked I began to see more of the black silhouettes taking shape. At first I felt confused because what I was looking at would not register in my brain. I had no point of reference. Everything I had ever spotted in these circumstances fell into a known category, but this shape could not be pigeonholed. My initial excitement slowly changed to confused irritation.

Moments passed and slowly one of the creatures stepped out into a sparse clearing in the foliage. There, about 75 yards away, was what I had only ever seen pictures of before that night, but there was absolutely no doubt in my mind I was looking at a small group of wild boar.

The rest, as they say, is history, and so started a long and fascinating association with these captivating creatures that I have observed, hunted, farmed and eaten ever since.

As with hunting any quarry, two essential prerequisites are: a good understanding of the species, and knowledge of the terrain in which the hunt is to take place.

Local knowledge is a valuable asset and information from the people, especially hunters who come from the area that you are hunting, should always be sought. A lot of information can be gleaned from books, magazines and the internet, but ultimately you cannot beat first-hand knowledge from someone who has been there and done it, so don't be too proud to ask.

THE QUARRY

As wild boars have no natural predators in the UK, hunting is the only way to regulate the population. Generally speaking, wild boar are nocturnal and so their presence is first suspected or even confirmed by damage to the ground, such as great lumps of turf being upturned or pheasant feeders having been raided, rather than sightings of the animal itself.

A group of wild boar or even a single beast in an area is not likely to go unnoticed, especially in arable areas, for example in southern England where the landscape might be slightly more manicured than in more remote areas of the country.

When wild boar are on the move they tend walk or even trot along at a good pace with their snout close to the ground, putting their keen sense of smell to good use. If the animal is able to sniff out food just below the surface it will stop and root around, causing the typical furrows in the ground that are seen when wild boar are present in an area.

Their presence is less obvious and certainly less damaging, some may even say beneficial, in large areas of woodland, for example in Scotland, where I have worked intensely with these creatures. It is believed that in this type of terrain their excavation work helps to aerate the soil.

Another indication of the presence of wild boar are footprints, but sadly, unless the hunter is proficient at recognising the spoor, it would be easy for them to be mistaken for other hoofed animals such as deer. There are of course some very obvious differences between a pig's footprint and that of sheep, cattle or deer, but as with all things in life understanding the difference comes with practice. All even-toed ungulates have a similar hoof structure, but the limb of a wild boar is distinctive in that its dew claws are set very low at the back and slightly to either side of the leg; they are also relatively large. This means that a clean track will clearly show two distinct impressions made by the dew claws to the rear and outside the cleaves or hoof.

The size of a footprint will obviously depend on the age and the sex of the animal that made it, but a really big boar may leave a print in the order of 10cm long.

The condition of the furrow made by rooting, or of the spoor left by a passing animal, will also give an indication of how long ago the track was made. For example, in damp soil, if the surface of the footprint

Large amounts of upturned turf – the result of the boar's foraging – will often be discovered before an actual sighting of boar

WILD BOAR – A BRITISH PERSPECTIVE 49

has dried out, this would be an indication that the imprint is not that recent. On the other hand a crisp print on wet ground makes it likely that the spoor is fresh. In wet, rainy conditions the sharpness of a track is very quickly eroded, making an estimation of how long ago the animal passed very difficult. Tracking any animal is a skill that will take a long time to master, and the only way to develop that skill is to get out there and practise at every opportunity.

My interest in tracking started many years ago while on an evasion course with the British army. I'll always remember a PSI telling me in the inimitable way that only an army instructor could: "Now you just listen to me, son, there are some f—g good trackers in the world, and if you want to stay one step ahead of them you had better listen to what I'm telling you." I did listen. I did learn, but I don't think I would ever have been able to stay one step ahead of some of the trackers that I have met since my army days; most notably some native African trackers. In most theatres of war the British army have either used trackers to locate the enemy or have been in situations where they have had to evade trackers working for the other side: the Boer war, Borneo, Malaya, Vietnam, Belize, and Afghanistan to name but a few. In the United States, the Pinkerton detectives, famous for hunting down Butch Cassidy and the Sundance Kid, used native American Indians led by Joe Lefors to follow their fugitives who were trying to evade capture. All of these trackers would have learned their skills by living close to the land and being able to read the signs.

My PSI described the ground as being like a blank sheet of writing paper, and every living thing and every inanimate object that moved across that ground was writing its own message about life in general and its own activity in particular. All the tracker has to do is read that message. As with any piece of literature, the reader has to be conversant with the language in which it is written, and a native speaker of a language may be aware of many different meanings in a piece of writing or even in the spoken word that a non native speaker may miss. As an example of what I mean, sarcasm, innuendo and the use of colloquialism may be lost when speaking English to a person of foreign origin. An individual may be taught to speak English, but only someone who has lived in an English-speaking country for some considerable time will have a real grasp of much of the language's hidden meaning. So too with what is written on the ground, only when a person grows up reading the signs that are in a constant state of change does that individual have a really true understanding of what has been written and is able to develop an instinctive feel for the story that nature is telling. Needless to say some men will be better at this than others.

A mature boar tends to live a more solitary life than the females and their young, who by necessity live in small groups or sounders. A boar will have a large territory, the size of which will depend on the availability of food, as well as habitat. The same may be said of family groups of sows and youngsters, except that the females are more likely to favour denser, smaller territories with more cover and therefore the careful observer may be able to detect more signs of their presence.

Paths or runs that are habitually used by small herds of boar may be found, which lead from daytime lairs to the animals' nocturnal feeding sites. Both the runs and the feeding places will be scattered with faeces, further confirmation that wild boar are present in the area.

Wild boar, like all pigs, love to wallow in mud holes, which serves as a means of ridding themselves of parasites, and regulating temperature, while some authorities believe it has a social function where the more dominant animal makes use of the mud bath before allowing subordinates to enter. After wallowing the beast then rubs itself against a tree as a final part of its cleansing routine. Tree rubbing is an activity that may be carried out by other animals in the forest, but the tell-tale dried mud on the trunk of a tree is a clear sign that it has been done by a wild boar. Wallows and dry mud on the trunk of a tree a foot or so above ground level therefore is more evidence of wild boar activity.

I recall one incident some years back when I was hot on the trail of a wild boar that was still within the confines of a very large fenced area, but that had escaped from a paddock while being transferred to a holding pen. With the help of my labrador, a bitch who was an expert at working with wild boar, I followed this itinerant beast over the hill and through head-high bracken for over an hour before it moved down to the banks of a wide river. I watched with interest from a high vantage point as the fugitive found some wet, silty shoreline mud and began to roll around in it. It would seem that he had decided that I was far enough behind him to afford him time to take this evasive action that might throw the dog off his scent. Interestingly the hog did not attempt to swim the river, despite the fact that wild boar are excellent swimmers.

PREPARING FOR THE HUNT

In the UK, hunting with hounds is not allowed and so the preferred method is to spot and stalk, or to make use of a high seat close to a well-used run where there has been a lot of recent activity. To go a step further on the latter method, where possible I would always try to bait the site for a few days prior to actually going out to shoot.

This serves two purposes; one is that if the bait is put out overnight, the most likely time for the animals to feed, it will tend to attract them to that spot and hold them there for a while. However, if, on inspection, the bait has not been touched, then clearly there are no wild boar in that area at this time. Trail cameras strategically placed around the high seat will be further confirmation of what is happening and at what time the animals might be expected to feed.

Compare the print of the red deer (top) to that of the boar where the dew claws are clearly visible

Chapter 3   HUNTING WILD BOAR IN BRITAIN: THE KNOWLEDGE

There is currently no closed hunting season for boar

In my opinion, where it is not possible to use dogs to flush the wild boar out of cover, by far the most successful method of shooting these creatures is at night, under a good moon, and over bait. Because of their usual behaviour of lying up in thick cover during the day and feeding at night, another method is to use beaters to flush them from their lair. There are, however, certain disadvantages.

In a large wood a lot of people are required in order to stand a good chance of being a sufficient threat to make the boar break cover, or indeed to prevent them breaking lines and running back past the beaters away from the guns. Added to this, unlike flushing birds with beaters (and dogs), this quarry is being pushed toward a much further reaching weapon. It is more likely that safety would be compromised, and therefore should only be done with the most meticulous planning and the strictest guidelines for both beaters and guns.

In Europe where hounds and beaters are used quite commonly, the beaters are able to keep well away from pegs where shooters are standing, letting the dogs venture into the riskier positions.

A spot and stalk approach to shooting wild boar is a far more opportunistic strategy, and success will only be achieved with lady luck playing a large part.

If a hunter was fortunate enough to happen upon a boar or group of boar out in the open, in broad daylight, and in an area that is appropriate for them to be shot, then it is a case of thanking St Hubert, Diana or whichever deity he pays homage to, and gettting on with the job in hand.

Realistically, however, simply going to an area that wild boar are known to inhabit and hoping to spot them and then engage them in a stalk is severely restricting one's chance of success.

In my opinion, all roads lead back to a baited site with a nearby high seat from which the hunter is able watch what goes on and can be far more discerning in what individual animal he is going take.

Currently the only legislation that applies to wild boar is that covered by The Animal Welfare Act 2006, The Wild Mammals (Protection) Act 1996, and the Wildlife and Countryside Act 1981; all of which are quite general in nature and are mainly concerned with protection against cruelty and unnecessary suffering, as well as the control and prevention of their release into the wild. There is also the Dangerous Wild Animals Act, which, as far as wild boar are concerned, simply deals with keeping them in captivity.

In practice, this means that there is no closed hunting season and all members of a herd are fair game. For most sportsmen, the practice of killing youngsters or pregnant and lactating sows is repugnant, and so the use of a high seat where a clear and unhurried assessment of the quarry can be made and an inappropriate kill avoided is another good reason why this method of hunting should be employed.

I have spent countless hours observing wild boar from a high seat and can attest to not only its worth in understanding the nature of these creatures, but also to its entertainment value.

Furthermore the sheer rush that is felt is unimaginable, when, after sitting in a cold hide for hours on end, suddenly one or more boar appears at the bait site. Sometimes they just seem to materialise from out of nowhere and on other occasions they can be heard scrimmaging around some while before they actually show themselves. Either way it is an experience that never fails to thrill.

Unless the wild boars are familiar with the bait site they tend to be hesitant about actually coming in to feed. They will circle around the area, often revealing glimpses of themselves in between trees, bushes or bracken, and will be heard grunting or foraging for any tasty morsel that might be found outside the clearing that is the bait station. It takes time for them to summon up enough courage to actually come out into the open.

When they do finally come out to feed it is often the younger adolescents that do so first, more mature animals did not get to that age by being reckless. However, when the older wild boar do come to eat they will unhesitatingly push the youngsters aside.

Wild boar, above all else, are social animals and a distinct hierarchy is seen within any group or sounder, never more so than when feeding. In a well organised group, in particular one that has not had its numbers reduced by over hunting or other

A spot and stalk approach is an opportunistic strategy, but it will work on occasion

WILD BOAR – A BRITISH PERSPECTIVE 53

Chapter 3 HUNTING WILD BOAR IN BRITAIN: THE KNOWLEDGE

Boar use mud baths to rid themselves of parasites and to regulate their temperature

interference from man, there will always be a dominant sow who will endeavour to look after the welfare of the others in her charge. She will be a mature animal, though neither necessarily the oldest nor the biggest, but she will command the respect of the other members of the group. In this naturally well-ordered sounder, should anything happen to the lead sow, such as death, injury or sickness. there will always be another sow, a second in command as it were, in the hierarchical structure ready to take her place.

The behaviour of wild boar at bait sites can be as varied as it is amusing. I have seen them during daylight hours quite happy to let magpies and crows sit on their backs, rooting around in the mammals coarse hair in the search for parasites or maybe just collecting a lining for their nests, I'm not sure which – although, as this happens at all times of the year I suspect it is not just for the latter.

The wild boar's good nature even extends to allowing deer to share their food. I have seen both roe deer and red deer feeding closely together with only the lightest of skirmishes taking place if one gets too close to the other. Although on one occasion things did get slightly rougher when a good sized red stag challenged a mature keiler for the right to feed there. In this case the stag, which was in hard antler, quickly gained the upper hand and the boar understandably gave the stag a suitably wide berth. Generally, however, if wild boar do not actually welcome visitors, they do at least seem to tolerate them.

On the other hand I have seen the mood change quite dramatically when a fox dared to stray too close. Charlie is quite definitely not welcome anywhere near a wild boar family and will be instantly chased off.

Another dark side of the wild boar psyche was observed as I watched a group feeding early one evening. It was a warm evening and the animals seemed quite peaceful, with the normal pushing and shoving as individual beasts vied for the best position or the tastiest morsel. Quietly, almost unnoticed at first, a young sow with two very small piglets at her side came into the feed area. I was not sure whether she was a part of this sounder or whether she was an outsider, but at first none of the other members of the group took any notice of her at all. She inched forward leaving her babies to watch her as she went to feed. I would have estimated these animals to have been around a week or 10 days old, probably no more. Suddenly the dominant sow rounded on the young female, pushed past her, and within seconds had despatched her offspring by biting them in half. Having lost her litter, it seemed that she was then accepted into the herd, for within five minutes she was feeding with the others.

Ironically, females within a sounder will usually share nursery duties and it is not at all uncommon for a sow to look after another sow's litter while the mother feeds or rests, but clearly on this occasion something was not quite right.

I have never seen a wild boar and a badger together in close proximity, but I have read Martin Goulding's account of just such a meeting and understand that there seemed to be a degree of mutual respect, with the badger ultimately being politely shown the door.

THE LAW

In order to own a firearm in the UK a firearm certificate (FAC) is necessary. This is a document issued to an applicant from the police authority in which the individual lives and will be dependent upon certain criteria, such as what the weapon is to be used for and if the applicant is a fit and proper person to be in possession of a firearm. In Britain there are only a limited number of reasons that are acceptable for owning a firearm with ammunition and, under normal circumstances, these are: membership of a shooting club, vermin control on a piece of land that is suitable for shooting and with the land owner's consent, or for stalking or sporting purposes, again with the land owner's permission. It will also be necessary to demonstrate that the firearms are to be kept in suitable gun safes, which are approved by the licensing authority.

Each individual gun that the issuing police force has given the FAC holder permission to own is entered onto the certificate, along with a reason for its use and amount and type of ammunition that the holder is authorised to keep.

If the purpose for which the firearm is used or the firearm itself is to be changed then a variation must be applied for and should be issued before the FAC holder takes any action.

In the case of wild boar, a variation should be sought that actually lists wild boar as a species that the holder is legally allowed to shoot. The licensing authority will normally want to know that wild boars are resident in the area that is being nominated before permission is given, and some authorities may even want to know what experience the applicant has of hunting these creatures.

Conversely I have heard of other authorities who are happy for their FAC holders to shoot wild boar under the conditions that are applied to vermin. It would also seem that these authorities are not concerned with the guidelines that have been issued in regard to appropriate calibres.

Because each police firearms licensing department appears to have its own interpretation of the various firearms and countryside acts, it's always the best policy to consult with your own licensing liaison officer before using your own firearm, as opposed to using an estate weapon, to take part in a wild boar hunt.

SAFE AND RESPONSIBLE HUNTING

As representatives of our sport we owe it to fellow hunters to act in a safe and courteous manner whenever we are in the field with a firearm. Nowadays there are all too many people ready to criticise not only hunting, but also the use of firearms and all that might entail. Certainly any encounter with the public while out searching for your quarry with a rifle thrown over your shoulder should be handled as tactfully as possible. Good manners cost nothing and politeness will go a long way in a situation that potentially could erupt into a heated debate (or worse) between what might be perceived as a tree hugging, bunny loving, vegetarian and a camo wearing butcher toting a high powered rifle and looking for all the world as though he has just stepped out of a video game. It is important to remember that the average member of the public has no dealings with firearms and will quite often be surprised to learn that the possession of a gun can in fact be perfectly legal.

In such an encounter all it would need is the sight of bloodied hands from a recent gralloch to send the average town dwelling dog walker in to a frenzy of such epic proportions that the ensuing drama would only be surpassed if the stalker proceeded to skin the mutt.

When out hunting, discretion and courtesy must always prevail along with what must be the ultimate prerequisite: safety. No sportsman should ever take a gun from his cabinet without having the following safety rules firmly and indelibly implanted in his mind:

1. Treat all firearms as though they are loaded.
2. Never point the firearm at anything that you do not want to shoot.
3. Do not touch the trigger until you have your sights on the target.
4. Positively identify your target before aiming at it and ensure that there is a safe backdrop behind your point of aim.
5. At all times ensure that your weapon is secure and not accessible to unauthorised individuals.

Whether I am stalking alone or guiding with a client, I will, in the case of a bolt action rifle, load the ammunition into the magazine and close the bolt over the top, leaving the breech empty. I will also, at the same time as closing the bolt, squeeze the trigger so that not only does the weapon have an empty breech, but it is not cocked either. The weapon is however, conveniently carrying a full payload of safely stored ammunition. When I am comfortably settled in position in my stand, hide or high seat, not having encountered my quarry on the way in, I will then chamber a round and ensure the safety catch is in the on position. Perfectly competent, safe and experienced stalkers may have slightly different thoughts on this subject, but they will all be based on reducing the possibility of an accidental or negligent discharge.

Only when the rifle is shouldered and pointing at the target should the safety be moved to the off position immediately prior to taking the shot.

In the case of a 'spot and stalk' style of hunt I would adopt the same technique, but

I would chamber a round when the quarry has been located. Again the safety would then be employed right up to the moment prior to the shot being taken.

In the case of single shot, double rifle or shotgun I would expect the weapon to be broken and an empty breech clearly visible until it is about to be used. The safety catch should be employed until the shot is taken. If a shoulder strap is used when walking with a firearm it should be carried with the barrel pointing straight up, or in the military style, pointing at the ground. It should not be waving around horizontally where it might inadvertently end up pointing at another member of the group. I have, on one or two occasions, been nervously aware that the client who is following in my footsteps has got a loaded weapon that appears to be waving around as though it has a mind of its own. My admonishment of these hapless individuals is normally followed by a degree of bad feeling.

CALIBRES AND TERMINAL BALLISTICS

Choosing the correct calibre to use when stalking wild boar may possibly be one of the most contentious issues to be discussed; and here is why.

If one reflects on the many variables such as size, speed, kinetic energy, momentum and type of bullet, there is no escaping the fact that above all else the single most important factor when making a clean kill is shot placement.

That said, if a number of different experts, both real and self-confessed, were asked to give their choice of calibre for the perfect wild boar round there would probably be just as many different points of view.

Most informed opinions will have a well thought out argument for their choice of calibre for any given game species, and with current trends and changing technology, I, for my part, am simply expressing my thoughts on a subject that has been debated long and hard for all of my 40 plus years of hunting and shooting, and will no doubt continue long after I have squeezed a trigger for the last time. I do not claim that my thoughts are definitive, simply a basis for debate.

Once a bullet has been accurately delivered to a chosen target area the rest is up to the terminal ballistics of the cartridge system to effect a clean kill. This is done by the bullet transferring its payload of kinetic energy into the vital organs of the animal being hunted.

The safety should be employed right up until the moment the shot is taken

Chapter 3 — HUNTING WILD BOAR IN BRITAIN: THE KNOWLEDGE

In my view, the idea that a bullet must release a predetermined level of energy in order to kill the game being hunted is fundamentally erroneous, and it must be stressed that it is a mistake to confuse knock down power with killing power.

The famous and prolific elephant hunter Walter 'Karamojo' Bell killed many of his 1,000 plus pachyderms with a Mannlicher Schoenauer chambered for .275 Rigby (7x57). Quite possibly madness, I agree, but in this respect Karamojo Bell could walk on water and his record proved it. It also proved that this small calibre gun was capable of laying to rest the biggest land mammal on Earth, which co-incidentally is why I chose the elephant as the model with which to make my point. I mention this as some readers may wonder why I should ramble on about elephants in a book dedicated to wild boar.

Even more outrageous than Karamojo's efforts are the stories that abound of these huge animals having been taken with .22 rimfire rifle, probably as a wager and quite definitely as an act of insanity. Yet it again makes the point that a tiny calibre releasing about 140ft/lbs of energy, in the right circumstances, can do the job.

I can almost hear the names that I am being called by the purists and disbelievers among the readers of this book for putting into print such blasphemy, but consider this.

A .458 Win Mag is a popular elephant round and one that I have used myself on many occasions. Although not everybody's choice, I am sure that there is no disputing its effectiveness when in an encounter with dangerous big game.

The .458 has a muzzle energy of approximately 5,000ft/lbs. The energy to animal weight ratio of a .458 to an elephant is about the same as a .22LR round to a fallow deer. So if we are happy to use a .458 on an elephant, why do we not use a .22 on deer, apart from the illegality of such an act of course?

The answer is that when it comes to bullets, knock down power does not exist. If our .458 bullet were to release its three tons' worth of kinetic energy on an inanimate 14-stone replica of a man it would fail to knock him over.

Living things fall when damage is caused by a bullet hitting tissue, causing limbs to break, blood vessels to rupture and vital organs to fail. A train hitting an animal will make it topple, but a bullet kills in a totally different way.

A .22LR bullet placed neatly into the ear hole of an elephant, or for that matter a wild boar, will have enough energy to penetrate the soft tissue that it will meet on its way to the equally soft brain where it will cause sufficient damage to 'knock' the animal down. Clearly in order to do this you have to be pretty sure of your marksmanship – and you will need two enormous orbs of soft tissue between your legs yourself to attempt this act of lunacy. Our .458 on the other hand has enough energy to penetrate less vulnerable, not so soft tissue in order to hit a vital organ.

What is needed then is a cartridge that will deliver enough energy to allow a bullet to penetrate the protective skin, bones and muscle and fatally damage a vital organ within the body cavity.

Energy is proportional to both the square of speed at which an object is moving and its mass.

From the equation $E = mv^2$ – where E is energy, m is mass and v^2 velocity squared – it can be seen that the energy that a bullet delivers can be increased by either making it bigger or faster.

Fast rounds have increased in popularity these days, partly because increasing the speed has a big effect on kinetic energy, but also because of the resulting flattening of the trajectory. Given that most hunters will be shooting their quarry at less than 200 metres, I sometimes feel that a bit too much emphasis is put on that aspect, certainly from the perspective of the pragmatic hunter and stalker rather than the long distance benchrest shooter or military sniper.

If we could be certain that every shot that was aimed at an animal was to hit a surface area that offered no resistance and that the bullet would reach the vital organs unimpeded, then the choice of calibre would be of very little concern, provided that the animal was within range. Clearly, however, this is not the case, so what is needed is a round that is able to reach inside the body of the animal and deliver its payload of energy into the vitals. This of course means breaking through the skin and bone.

There are many hunters who would say that, without a doubt, size matters and a true measure of killing power is momentum. A big bullet, even though it is travelling relatively slower than its lighter counterpart, may well have more momentum.

Opinions generally differ between those who believe that a high striking velocity, and therefore a high kinetic energy, is everything, and those who feel that a greater bullet weight with more momentum is the mark of effectiveness.

My final thought on the subject of terminal ballistics is concerned with the composition of the bullet being used. The manufacturing of bullets is a precise science, but their construction may differ from one to the other. Some are made of solid brass or lead, while others will have hollow points or lead cores with metal jackets. A more recent design, thanks primarily to the inventiveness of John Nosler, is the partition bullet. The central core divides on impact into petals that, due to the rifling inside the firearm's barrel, spin and tear through tissue like a runaway propeller, causing maximum trauma to vital organs.

The intention of all of these designs is that, first of all, they are capable of deep penetration. Then, with the exception of the solid bullets, they expand once inside the body cavity and retain most of their mass. In other words, the bullet should stay in one piece and not fragment inside the target.

For sheer killing power, most people, I think, would agree that it is best to go for a heavier bullet, which, as I have already said, as a rule tends to be slower. A slow moving

Example of the trajectory of a Winchester .308 with a muzzle velocity of 2810 fps

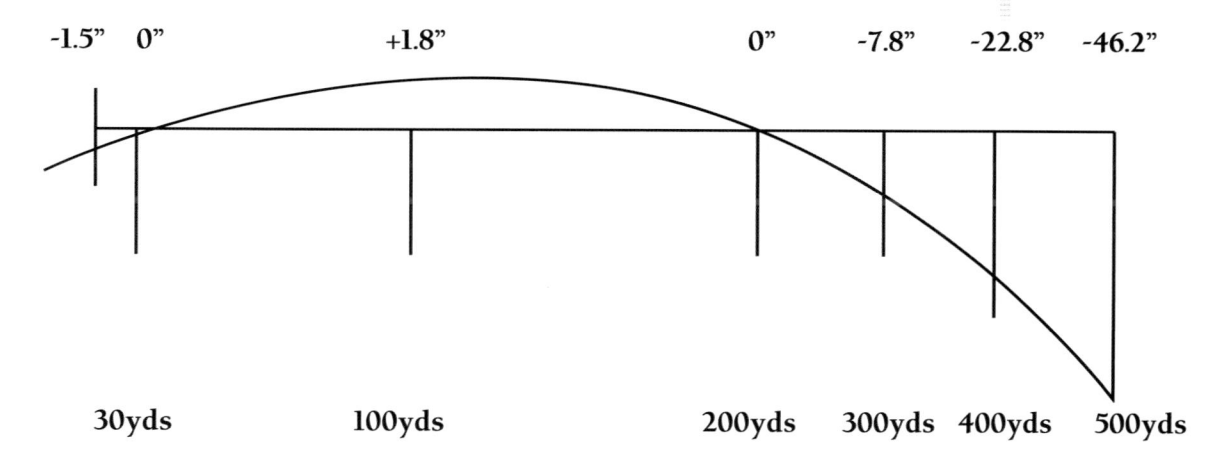

-1.5"   0"   +1.8"   0"   -7.8"   -22.8" -46.2"

30yds   100yds   200yds 300yds 400yds 500yds

Without elevation

Sight Line

Trajectory

With elevation

Trajectory

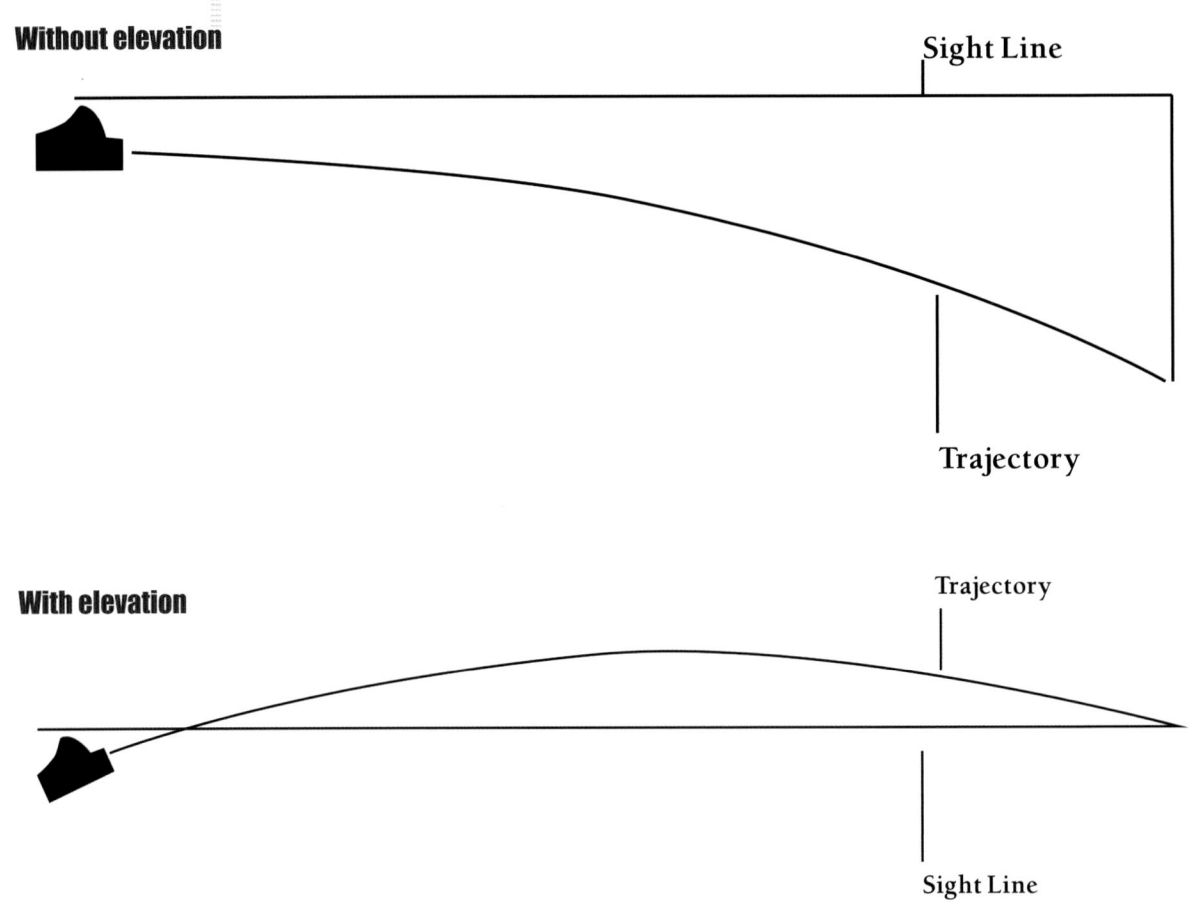

Sight Line

bullet will make an exit wound barely larger than its point of entry, whereas a faster bullet will cause a larger exit wound and quite likely more meat damage.

When choosing a cartridge it is important to consider kinetic energy, but I do not believe that is always the dominant issue. Sometimes a given situation may require less energy. By this I mean that a bullet that passes straight through a body will have plenty of energy, but it will take that energy with it when it passes out through the other side of the animal – it is therefore wasted.

If the weight and velocity of two rounds were identical, then the bullet that expands the most will penetrate the least, and of course the converse is also true. Therefore, like so many other things in life that I have reflected upon, I believe that calibre, bullet mass and velocity is very much a matter of compromise.

TRAJECTORY

Every shooter knows what trajectory is, and most believe that they understand it, but we have all heard a tale or two where a hunter missed the trophy of a lifetime because he did not put his understanding of the trajectory of his bullet into practice.

Pages, if not whole volumes, could and have been written on the physics of the flight paths or trajectories of projectiles. However what we need to understand as riflemen is how to apply this data in practical terms. In other words, how to make use of our understanding of trajectories.

Trajectory is the curved path of a projectile's flight. However the practicalities of trajectory as described in this simple definition are far more complicated than the theoretical movement of a ball travelling through a vacuum.

The path of a bullet as it leaves the muzzle of a rifle will be subjected to many influences while it is in flight. To name but a few, our projectile, the bullet, is an elongated rigid body subjected to rapid rotation, which makes both temperature and air resistance a significant factor. Gravity is a constant factor, but the time during which the gravitational force is acting on that body and the distance travelled will vary depending on the elevation of the barrel.

Every shot fired from a rifle will hit its target at only two distances along its flight path, but the one that we are interested in is the most distant: our point of aim or striking point. Notice on the diagram on the previous page how the projectile will hit the target at only two distances

It is important to understand that the moment the bullet leaves the muzzle it starts to fall and despite the fact that it will be travelling at thousands of feet per second, it will drop at the same rate as if you had just let it fall out of your hand.

In other words, a bullet fired horizontally from a rifle will hit the ground hundreds of yards away at exactly the same time as a bullet that had been balanced on the end of the same barrel and fell directly to the floor as the rifle was fired.

In its simplest form, without taking into account air resistance, the bullet drop can be expressed mathematically by the following equation: Drop = $\frac{1}{2}g\,T^2$, where g is gravity in feet per second and T is time of flight in seconds.

Clearly then, depending upon the distance at which the weapon is sighted in, the elevation of the muzzle will need to be altered for different points of aim to allow for bullet drop or trajectory.

Familiarity with your weapon and ammunition will ensure that even though your rifle is sighted in at a given distance, providing you are aware of the trajectory of the round that you are using, you are able to accurately compensate for a target situated beyond or within that distance.

POINT BLANK RANGE

There are three definitions of the expression point blank range. The first is not really a definition so much as the common misuse of a technical term. Some shooters,

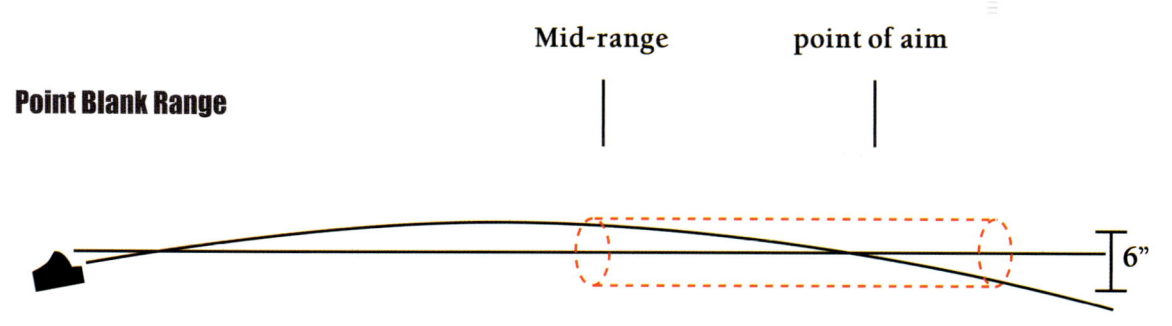

Point Blank Range

Mid-range   point of aim

Circles showing area over target in point blank range which extends approximately 20% beyond the point of aim

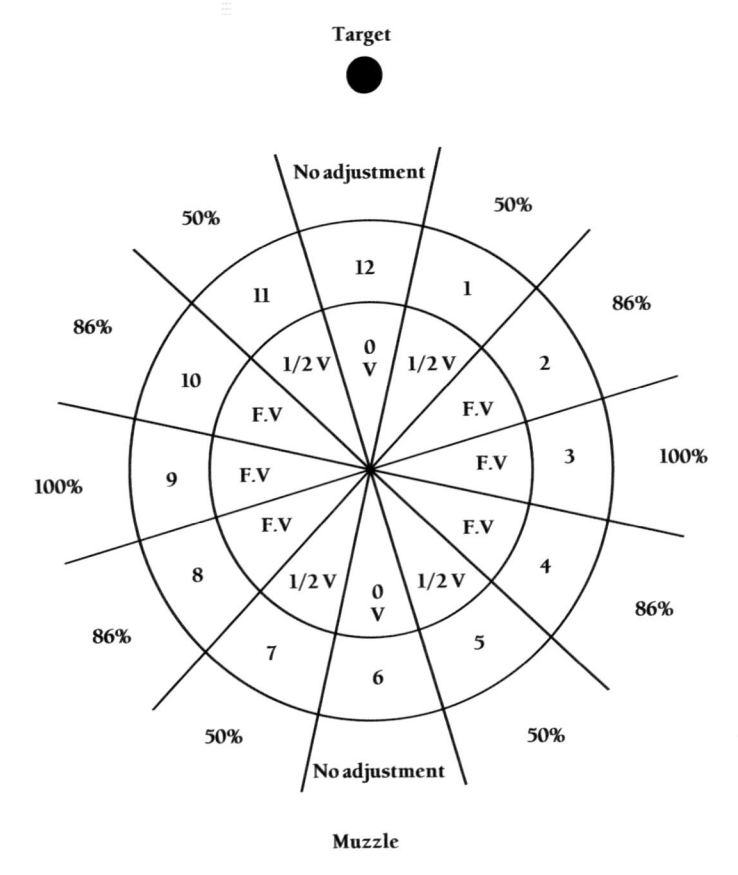

Chapter 3 — HUNTING WILD BOAR IN BRITAIN: THE KNOWLEDGE

Target

```
                  No adjustment
         50%          12         50%
              11            1
     86%                              86%
          10    1/2 V  0  1/2 V   2
                  V
                F.V      F.V
   100%     9   F.V        F.V    3   100%
                F.V        F.V
                F.V      F.V
            8   1/2 V  0  1/2 V   4
                       V
     86%                              86%
              7             5
         50%          6         50%
                  No adjustment
                    Muzzle
```

Wind positions and deflection effect

and most of the non-shooting public with no knowledge of firearms, believe that point blank range is an unspecified distance, but one that is very close to the muzzle. It becomes a colloquialism used to describe a target that is very close. That's OK for a conversation at the pub, but it's wholly inaccurate.

The first true meaning of point blank range is used to describe the first downrange distance that requires no elevation change to hit the point of aim. It is the first point of aim, which will be just tens of yards away, even though the primary point of aim or target is usually 100 or 200 yards away. In other words it is the point at which the projectile first crosses the line of sight. This is a correct meaning of the term, but it is not often used in this context.

The most meaningful and commonly used definition of the phrase point blank range is the maximum distance that will result in an accurate hit in a vital area with the sights set on the target and without considering the bullet's drop.

In the case of a wild boar, if we consider the target to be an abstract circle over the animal's heart, then the point blank range will be the range of distances along the bullet's trajectory where the bullet would strike within that circle.

If the diameter was six inches, then the sights would be adjusted for the range that would not let the bullet pass more than three inches above or below the centre of that circle. For maximum point blank range the sights should be adjusted by sighting in at that range for which the maximum ordinate is three inches above the line of sight. Practically, this will be equal to the midrange trajectory height. Computer ballistic programmes will compute the point blank range providing we have the necessary data to feed in to it. Information required will be the diameter of the target area, which is obviously different for different game, the ballistic coefficient of the ammunition being used, and the muzzle velocity.

As a rough estimate, the point blank range for a sporting rifle can be taken as 20 per cent further than the weapon is sighted-in.

The big question is, will changing the sight-in range to point blank range help the hunter kill his wild boar? Possibly. It will help slightly to compensate for errors in range estimation and sight adjustment.

Windage

This is the science, or maybe I should say

the art of lateral sight adjustment and must be one of the hardest skills in shooting to master, partly because there are so many variables – and even the variables are variable.

Take, for example, wind speed and direction. It is difficult enough for the average man to determine the speed of the wind as it blows in his face, but even if he is able to do that accurately, he can only guess at its speed at the target which maybe 500 yards away and may be in a more sheltered position.

Without the use of anemometer, which is anything but a convenient tool to use, 'doping the wind', that is guessing the wind speed and calculating the angle of deflection, is, to say the least, difficult.

The following approximations maybe helpful:

1. A wind speed of one or two miles per hour is calm and can be ignored
2. Three to six miles per hour is a light breeze; noticeable, but it will not be a problem to, as an example, light a match
3. Seven to 12 miles per hour is beginning to get strong; lighting a match will require a shield
4. At 15 miles per hour watch your hat doesn't blow off
5. At 20 miles per hour an accurate shot at long range will require a good deal of skill
6. At 25 miles per hour or more make sure your boar is pretty damn close or call it a day.

Wind direction can also be misleading and may be coming from one orientation at the muzzle, but can be different at the target as a result of mini air currents or eddies immediately around the point of aim.

Added to this, bullet weight and speed have to be programmed in to the equation in order to work out the adjustment needed to compensate.

FACTORS AFFECTING THE LATERAL PATH OF A BULLET

The crosswind angle

In long distance shooting, bullet deflection caused by even a light wind is likely to cause bigger problems than elevation errors. The severity of deflection can be simplified by regarding the direction from which the wind is coming as having full value, half value or zero value. In military terms, wind coming from two, three, four, eight, nine and 10 o'clock positions have full value; winds from one, five, seven and 11 o'clock have half value; and winds from six and 12 o'clock have zero value. Therefore a 20-miles-per-hour wind coming from the one o'clock position will have a half value, and so be equivalent to a 10 miles per hour wind.

Time

Clearly the longer the time that a bullet is travelling between the muzzle and the target the greater exposure it will have to the influence of the wind. Therefore the greater the distance of the shot, the more the bullet will drift off target. All things being equal, the deflection will be directly proportional to the time it is in the air.

Weight

This factor is important because, due to an object's momentum, the heavier it is the more difficult it is to push of course.

Velocity

A slow, heavy bullet has most resistance to a change of direction caused by the wind. For the science behind that, read on. If a light bullet and a heavy bullet are shot at the same time, but at the same momentum, this means the light bullet has to have a a faster velocity than the heavier bullet (momentum = mass x velocity). Therefore the lighter bullet will lose speed at a greater rate and thus the heavier bullet is thrown off-course less.

If the velocity of the lighter bullet were raised so that its momentum is higher than the slower, heavy bullet, the lighter bullet will be moved less by the crosswind.

In this situation however, the lighter bullet will not be able to hold its velocity compared to the heavy bullet that will hold it quite well. At some distance along their trajectories, the lighter bullet will lose its momentum to the point where it loses its advantage

Ballistic coefficient
This is an index of a given bullet's ability to overcome air resistance in flight. A full explanation of the ballistic coefficient is beyond the scope of a book on hunting wild boar, but would be worth further research for anybody with more than a modicum of interest in ballistics.

Although all of the above have a practical influence on the path of a bullet exposed to a crosswind, it must be said that the ballistic coefficient and high velocity are the main factors in reducing wind deflection.

In summary then, there are a number of different formulae for calculating wind deflection, all of which can be impossible to use at that moment when your head is spinning with the anticipation of a shot and your heart is pumping adrenaline round your body at a rate that makes you think it is about to burst.

I recall a friend of mine, a pronghorn hunter from Alabama, called 'Lucky' Bailey who used a workable guide that was not too difficult to remember in times of stress. He gave me this advice soon after he had successful killed a pronghorn at the best part of 1,000 yards on the prairies of Wyoming.

If you are shooting 180-grain 30-06 bullets at 2,700 fps and a 10 miles per hour wind is coming at right angles, allow one inch at 100 yards, two inches at 200 yards, six inches at 300 yards and 12 inches at 400 yards. If the wind is coming at 45 degrees instead of 90, halve these figures, and if the wind is at 20mph then double them. He never told me what he did for his pronghorn at 1,000 yards, but if I recall it was a dead calm day.

Just to emphasise the complexity of the problem of wind deflection, I recall many years ago being on a rifle range in Wales. I was in the military and being instructed by a sniper from the Royal Green Jackets who made shooting at long distance look easy. One of the lads asked him how he was able to judge the wind adjustment so easily. "Oh it's quite simple really," replied the Royal Green Jacket. You just watch 20,000 or so rounds of 7.62mm go down the range and you get to know. Mind you if it were any other calibre I wouldn't have a clue." I am sure he was being overly modest, but you get the point.

SHOOTING UP OR DOWN HILL
A shot fired up or downhill will always be high unless compensated for, which means the shooter must aim low. The reason being that the force of gravity is at its strongest when acting perpendicular to a body. A bullet fired at any angle up or down will be subjected to less gravitational pull and therefore stay higher for longer.

To compensate, simple trigonometry is needed to calculate the equivalent horizontal distance. As an example, a shot fired at a 45 degree angle at a target 300 yards away will have an equivalent horizontal distance of 210 yards. The shot should therefore be aimed at the target as if it were at 210 yards not 300.

There are several methods of calculating how to compensate for shooting at an angle including using bullet drop data and, multiplying the amount of drop in inches by a compensation factor. However these types of calculation are impossibly difficult in the field.

A method that is employed by some police and military units is known as the 'quick fix method' and is to some extent a compromise, but it can be calculated very quickly. Based on just three angles, 30 degrees, 45 degrees and 60 degrees, the method is to aim at a percentage of the distance to the target for any given angle, as follows: 30 degrees, 90 per cent; 45 degrees, 70 per cent; and 60 degrees, 50 per cent. Therefore, in the example cited above, for a target at 45 degrees placed 300 yards away the compensation will be 70 per cent of 300 yards, which is 210 yards. In this example the rifleman will be aiming low to hit a target at 300 yards that is being treated as though it were only 210 yards away.

Compensation becomes infinitesimally small when the angle at which the shot

There are plenty of calculations that need to take place before a clean shot can be taken

Chapter 3: HUNTING WILD BOAR IN BRITAIN: THE KNOWLEDGE

is being made is small, and it is unlikely that while shooting wild boar that such calculations will need to be made. This is more of a problem for the goat hunter or when stalking red deer on the open hill.

So having waded through my esoteric ramblings on external ballistics what conclusion do we arrive at? What is the perfect calibre rifle with which to humanely kill a wild boar?

TYPES OF FIREARM AND AMMUNITION

It is normal practice in the UK to use a rifle in the pursuit of wild boar, although it is not unlawful to use a shotgun. However there are some clearly laid out guidelines by a number of different authorities – including The Deer Initiative, an organisation funded by such government departments as DEFRA and the Forestry Commission, as well as the British Association for Shooting and Conservation (BASC), one of Britain's leading shooting organisations – on the calibre of weapons to be used for hunting wild pigs.

A rifle should not be smaller than a .270, using nothing less than a 150-grain expanding bullet. In most European countries .30cal rifles are preferred, with the classic wild boar round being a 9.3x54R. I think it would be fair to say that most of the wild boar that I have hunted over the years, and that number is now quite considerable, have been taken with a .308Win, and more often than not using a 150-180-grain partition bullet.

I am a great fan of ballistic tips, which on lighter, softer skinned deer and antelope works really well, but on tough skinned wild boar I just feel slightly more comfortable with the partition bullet. Critics may say that the partition bullet is good until it hits bone, when it may mushroom out too quickly thus failing to achieve adequate penetration. I have never found this to be a problem and, as always, shot placement is of paramount importance – a well-placed bullet avoids the need for the missile to have to punch its way through heavy bone tissue.

Shotguns may be used to kill wild boar, but again the guidelines are quite clear in how they should be used. For what it's worth, I personally feel that except under certain conditions, namely at extremely close quarters, a shotgun does not provide the shooter with enough latitude to deal with the innumerable assortment of conditions and targets that may present themselves when stalking or even hunting these animals from a stand or high seat.

Again the law does not specifically cover the use of shotguns when shooting boar, but the following should be considered essential. The shotgun should be a minimum of a 12 gauge with at least a three-inch chamber. It should be a multi-shot weapon, whether that's a double barrelled gun or semi-auto and ideally should be fully choked. Cartridges should be of the AAA or SSG type. Solid rifled slugs may be used, but remember this type of ammunition, or any cartridge using a load of less than five shots or with individual shot measuring bigger than 0.36 inches, requires a FAC and cannot be used on a shotgun certificate.

There is no law against shooting boar with a shotgun, but most hunters in Britain favour a rifle

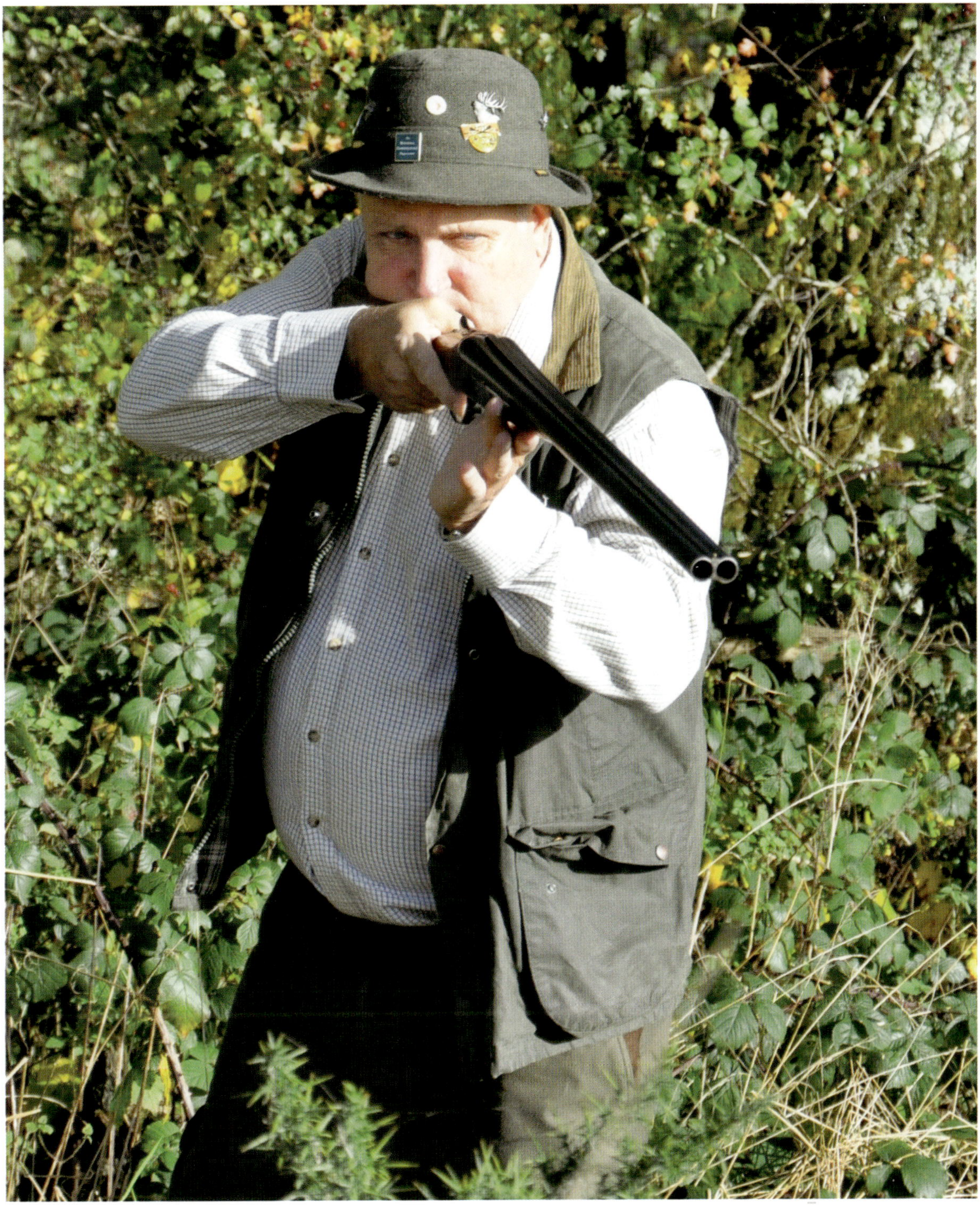

HUNTING WILD BOAR IN BRITAIN: THE EQUIPMENT

RIFLES

The make of rifle, as opposed to the calibre, is of course very much a matter of personal choice where many factors need to be taken into consideration, not least of which may well be the cost.

The list of manufacturers is vast and it is not the intention of this publication to persuade the reader to choose one model over another, but rather to encourage further research into the myriad options open to the hunter and stalker. To this end I have included several reviews of popular rifles, which the reader may find helpful or of interest. Only after reading reviews, asking the opinion of fellow sportsmen, and, where possible, testing potential purchases on the range or in the field, can an informed decision be reached.

Names that come to mind when considering a good, reliable weapon for the pursuit of wild boar are: Mauser, Winchester, Remington, Ruger, Blaser, CZ, Browning, Heym, Steyr Mannlicher, not to mention double rifles from Krieghoff and Chapuis, or classic English guns, such as Holland and Holland, James Purdey and Westley Richards.

As well as deciding what make of firearm to have, the prospective purchaser will also have to choose its configuration. Commonly there are three types seen on hunts in Europe, these are the bolt action, the double rifle and the combination or drilling rifle/shotgun. The shotgun is not often used for wild boar in Europe, but when it is it will usually be loaded with a solid slug, the most well-known of which is the Brenneke.

In the UK, by far and away the most commonly used firearm is the bolt action rifle, although without a doubt the sportsman who turns up at a wild boar hunt with a double rifle will be the centre of attention. A shotgun on the other hand, while being perfectly legal, is more likely be more frowned upon than appreciated.

Combination rifles are useful when hunting wild boar or deer in case a fox or other ground or winged vermin should turn up unexpectedly, but in truth they are a bit of a rarity on such events in the UK.

Bolt action magazine rifles

The majority of sporting rifles used in the UK are of this type. Bolt actions first appeared on single-shot guns, but were soon adapted for use as a mechanism for repeating rifles.

The magazine may be either integral, which by definition is an ammunition reservoir contained within the rifle and is not readily removed; or a detachable magazine, which is a removable container and is manually loaded with cartridges and then fitted into the magazine well of the rifle.

It may be of interest to some readers that the old military Lee Enfield rifle, which since its heyday as the standard infantry weapon of the British army has been popularly sporterised, uses a magazine system that is in some ways mid-way between those described above.

The 10-shot removable box magazine may be loaded out of the rifle, as in the case of a detachable magazine, or alternatively ammunition may be fed through the top of the receiver and into the magazine while it is in situ.

With this type of firearm, ammunition is fed into the breech from the magazine by the action of the bolt which then ejects a spent cartridge before reloading a new one.

The traditional bolt action has the same turn and slide operating principle as a shed door bolt, and most modern systems are based on the Mauser model 98, although much more recently straight pull mechanisms have become popular.

These newer innovations, designed again by Mauser in their 96 model and another by Blaser in their model R93, were the result of hunters wanting a slicker, faster action especially when going for a second shot on driven game. These systems do away with the rotational movement of

Attending a boar hunt with a double rifle will ensure that you are the centre of attention

Chapter 4 — HUNTING WILD BOAR IN BRITAIN: THE EQUIPMENT

Image credit: Nick Latus

The fine boar engraving on this double rifle is a sign of its princely status

the bolt in the breech and instead the bolt is simply worked back and forth making reloading a marginally quicker and smoother process.

Double rifles

Many would argue that the double rifle is the princely star among sporting rifles, a status that is reflected in the price tag that is normally attached to such weapons.

Double rifles are, or at least were, quintessentially British, and their origins go back to the early part of the 19th century. They were developed for the well-heeled hunter who sought excitement and glory in pursuit of big game in the far flung and often unexplored corners of the mighty British Empire. In those far off days a double rifle built by one of the great English gun makers was symbolic of what put the Great in Britain and its owner would carry it with pride.

In appearance the double rifle closely resembles a shotgun, whether it is an over-and-under or a side-by-side, the obvious and clear difference being the rifled barrels of the former as opposed to the smooth bore of shotgun barrels.

There are a number of advantages in using a double rifle, not least of which is the speed with which a second shot may be fired. There is also the safety aspect where the weapon can not only be made safe by being carried in the break-open position, but it can clearly be seen by other hunters that the weapon poses no danger. Being able to quickly swing onto running game, along with reliability, are factors that makes the double rifle a serious contender as the weapon of choice for wild boar.

However there are one or two points that make the double rifle less than number one on the list. Firstly the cost of building an accurate double, capable of consistently placing bullets into a tight group at 100 yards is staggering. Joining two barrels that produce the same point of impact is a skill that only few gunsmiths have mastered and can be quite a lengthy process. At 100 yards each barrel should be able to place a bullet within six inches of the other and high end manufacturers will strive for much better. Generally speaking, however, the most commonly cited criticism of the double rifle is its inaccuracy at anything more than 50 yards.

Settling for cheaper, inferior versions of these beautiful, iconic firearms should not be an option and quality should not be compromised because of price; it's far better to go for a good, affordable bolt action rifle than an 'economic' double.

The drilling or combination gun

As the name implies, this gun employs the use of both the smooth bored barrels of a shotgun and the rifled barrel of a firearm. Although classically this combination will be two smooth 12 bore barrels and a single 7x54R or even a 9.3x75R rifled barrel, this does not necessarily have to be the case. The combinations and number of barrels are numerous, as indeed are the calibres used.

Shotguns

I am not a great advocate of the use of shotguns for shooting wild boar, but when used with a solid slug or AAA or SSG cartridges they are a choice if held on a (section one) firearm certificate and therefore deserve a mention.

The once traditional side-by-side shotgun seems to be slowly getting replaced by the increasingly popular over-and-under models, but either one should be used without a choke when using a solid shot. Some manufacturers actually make shotguns that are specifically designed to be used with solid ammunition, the barrels of which are regulated to have a common point of impact at 50 yards.

An alternative to double barrelled shotguns is the pump action gun, which in the UK is limited to three shots if being used on a shotgun certificate, even so the solid slug ammunition still requires a FAC.

I believe that the use of shotguns of all types is far more popular in France than in other mainland European countries and I have only rarely encountered their use in the UK.

RIFLE OPTICS

Just as with the rifles upon which they sit, there are a multitude of riflescopes to choose from, and as a rifle's optics may well cost more than the firearm with which they are to be used, it is important to make the right choice.

For more years than I care to remember I have read articles in popular magazines reviewing or sometimes comparing the merits of one scope over another. I often question whether the authors of some of these words of wisdom really have an understanding of optical physics or if they have simply been led by the latest marketing hype of the manufacturer whose product they are considering. I am not putting myself up here as the ultimate expert by any means, but what I am saying is don't take it for granted that just because

Chapter 4 — HUNTING WILD BOAR IN BRITAIN: THE EQUIPMENT

This Swarovski scope offers variable zoom up to 6x with a 24mm objective lens – a good combination for wild boar

it is in printed form you must be reading the whole truth. Always question what you are being told and choose your source of information carefully - that includes what you are reading now.

I also believe that very often the brochures issued by manufacturers advertising their products can be misleading. I am thinking here of how the maker will put a spin on one aspect or another, regardless of whether or not that particular feature has any practical benefit. Take for example how the popular trend currently seems to be towards a large objective lens or excessive magnification and yet, for reasons that I will explain, they may well be quite counterproductive.

Riflescopes are typically referred to by the use of two numbers separated by an 'x'. An example might be 4x32. The first number refers to the magnification, which means in the case of a 4x scope the object being viewed appears to be four times closer than viewed with the unaided eye.

The second number in the formula (4x32) is the diameter of the objective lens or front lens in millimetres. In this case 32mm. Certainly the size of an objective lens is important because it controls the amount of light that enters the scope and therefore reaches your eye. What is not usually highlighted is that a large front lens means a much bigger and heavier scope. Another drawback with a large diameter objective lens is concerned with the so called exit pupil, which I will discuss in a moment.

Clearly a high magnification is a good selling point for the makers of riflescopes, but rarely if ever is it mentioned that this feature will compromise such optical characteristics as field of view, depth of field, chromatic aberration, eye relief and again exit pupil, all of which may be desirable qualities in an optical system.

As controversial as this may seem, I believe that in medium to high power scopes the largest objective lens that will normally be needed is 40mm, and in low powered scopes 32mm is as big as it needs to be.

The amount of light that gets to the eye is in fact determined by the exit pupil rather than the objective lens – the former can be seen by holding the scope at arm's length and looking through the eyepiece. The small illuminated circle seen in the middle of the ocular lens is the exit pupil and its size can be calculated by dividing the diameter of the objective lens by the power or magnification. In the case of the 4x32 scope, the exit pupil is 8mm.

If the scope were a variable 4-12x40 instrument, then at the more powerful end of its range the exit pupil would be 40 divided by 12 or 3.33mm. This is not a problem so long as the ambient light is sufficient to enable the pupil of the eye to be smaller than the exit pupil. In the poor light of dusk the human eye will attempt to compensate by dilating and if the eye pupil becomes larger than 3.33mm then the exit pupil becomes a limiting factor rendering the scope inefficient.

It should be mentioned that a healthy human eye can have a dilated pupil measuring in 7mm, which puts the 3.33mm exit pupil of the 12x40 scope into perspective – you may actually be better off without the scope.

On the other hand, the 4x40 scope with an exit pupil of 8 mm is larger than the human pupil and so will never limit what you can see, even when the light has faded beyond dusk or before dawn.

If the objective lens were bigger, let's say a 4x52, there is no doubt that exit pupil would bigger, 13mm in fact, but in this case it would be so much more than the human eye can make use of as to render it useless.

The human eye adapts to changing light conditions, but, like everything else, becomes less efficient with age, so that by middle age the pupil will dilate to a maximum of about 5mm (no longer 7mm) and in old age even less.

Large objective lenses come into their own when hunting at long distances at high magnifications for quarry such as pronghorn antelope when the light is fading. A good example of such a scope is the Zeiss Victory FL Diavari that comes with a 72mm objective lens and 24x magnification. This is an exceptional scope, but definitely not for pigs.

An important feature to look for when choosing a scope for shooting wild boar is a wide field of view, which technically is measured in degrees, although is often described by the linear area covered by the instrument. The field of view may be defined as the diameter across a circular field at a given distance, which may be the number of feet at 100yards or metres at 100metres. Because the field of view is actually measured in degrees it follows that the closer the object is to the lens the smaller that area will be.

For the hunter who spends a lot his time in the woods or who may have to lock on to a running target (not to be recommended), a wide field of view is essential. However, be warned, the field of view is inversely proportional to the magnification as the following example will attest.

A 3-9x variable scope, with a linear field of view of 32 feet at 100yards when set at 3x magnification, will only have a 14 feet field of view when the scope is used on the higher 9x power setting. A rule of thumb might be to keep a variable scope on a low power unless circumstances dictate otherwise, or simply use a lower, fixed power scope.

Common adjustments on scopes: digital controls for illuminated reticles (top) and finger turrets for windage and elevation (bottom)

WILD BOAR – A BRITISH PERSPECTIVE 73

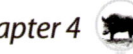

Chapter 4 — HUNTING WILD BOAR IN BRITAIN: THE EQUIPMENT

So, we are now beginning to build up a profile of the ideal scope for wild boar.

First of all we want a large objective lens, but not one that is so big as to adversely affect the exit pupil. We also want a degree of magnification, but not so much that it will limit the field of view or again have a negative effect on the exit pupil. Finally, with what we have looked at so far, we need a scope that will allow us a good area of vision, which is made possible by choosing carefully the properties that have already been detailed above.

What would make an ideal set of optics for wild boar would be a simple, inconspicuous, good all-round scope with a fixed 6x42 or maybe a variable 3-9x36 or 3-12x42 specification.

For many years the 4x scope was considered a good all-round scope, ideal for the woods and yet adequate on the hill. Low powered scopes are quite hard to find these days and have largely been replaced by variable 1-4x or a 2-7x. Certainly if the scope is to be used on more than one type of quarry or in different terrain where magnification or the field of view may need to be altered, it is much more desirable to change this by the turn of a ring than a change of scopes.

Of course there are many other considerations to take into account when choosing a riflescope for your own personal requirements, an understanding of the following is important.

The reticle

The reticle or crosshairs are the intersecting lines that are seen when looking through a riflescope. They come in many guises, including:

Wire reticles – fine wires that may be flattened to varying degrees of thickness. They are usually silver, but appear black when they are backlit by the image that is being viewed. The centre section of the crosswire is left unflattened, leaving a fine, hair-like cross, which is centred over the target and is narrow enough not to block out the image. This is known as a duplex reticle, and was invented by Leupold and is fast becoming the most popular type of crosshair.

Etched reticles – in this reticle a diamond-etched glass replaces the crosshairs and allows for the easy addition of features such as bullet drop compensation lines during the manufacturing process.

Illuminated reticles – for use in poor light conditions. They collect ambient light through fibre optics or by battery powered LEDs, and, as the name implies, illuminate the reticle, which would otherwise be obscured by the dark target in failing light. Critics of this type of reticle have two main areas of complaint. One is that 'legal light' for most game is half an hour before sunrise and half an hour after sunset. However, *Outdoor Life* conducted a test and concluded that all but the poorest quality optics are bright enough to enable vital areas to be seen even after legal light has gone. The other criticism is that anything but the very faintest illumination on the reticule will ruin your night vision. Personally I have found these scopes useful, but it is for the intended purchaser to research further before splashing out the extra cost.

Bullet drop compensating reticles – also known as range compensating

74 WILD BOAR – A BRITISH PERSPECTIVE

reticles. These have lines that enable the user to compensate for bullet drop if the target is beyond the distance that the rifle has been sighted in at. Many popular scopes have this feature built-in nowadays.

Eye relief
This is the distance between the ocular lens and the eye, and it is important to get this right if injury is to be avoided when the scope is mounted on a centrefire rifle. On a rifle that produces a lot of recoil the eye relief should be longer and on these larger calibre firearms it should be between three and five inches.

Parallax
This refers to the apparent movement of the target relative to reticle, dependent on the point of observation. It probably causes most concern because the line of sight of the scope is different to that of the bore of the rifle.

Parallax is minimised by mounting the scope as close to the barrel as is practicable.

Red-dot scopes
The red-dot sighting system is a short, squat scope containing battery powered electronics that project a dot at the point of aim in the tube in place of the crosshairs. This sort of sight has conventional turrets for adjusting windage and elevation, but has no magnification.

The optics put the image of the target and the red dot in the same optical plane, but because of the long eye relief and zero magnification the dot does not need to be focused, unlike the reticule in a conventional scope. This type of sight is very light in weight and the small batteries last a long time before needing to be replaced.

Because this type of sighting system is used by keeping both eyes open along with the zero magnification, target acquisition can be very rapid, ideal for moving game and poor lighting conditions. This is certainly a system worth considering for hunting wild boar.

Quality
The saying 'You only get what you pay for' applies to good optics as much as it does to anything else, but in this case the better design and quality of components that go into the more expensive products more than justifies the extra cost.

The quality of glass, the method used in polishing, and the coatings that are applied to the lenses will all affect the performance of the scope and therefore the price.

Quite often the brand name is a good guide to the quality of optics that you might consider buying.

Companies like Zeiss, Swarovski, Leupold and Schmidt & Bender, among others, have built a reputation over many years for producing high quality goods and are not likely to sell an inferior product.

On the other hand there are a number of companies that produce perfectly good products, but are aimed at the less prestigious end of the market; these are companies such as BSA, Bushnell and Tasco.

Top: A red-dot is useful for rapid target acquisition

Top left: An example of an illuminated reticle

Chapter 4 — HUNTING WILD BOAR IN BRITAIN: THE EQUIPMENT

RIFLE REVIEWS

The Mauser Model 03

Wilhelm and Paul Mauser founded the Mauser weapons factory in 1874, and to this day it enjoys worldwide fame and has a name synonymous with firearm quality. The brothers began their work as children, as did their father, in the royal weapons factory in Oberndorf/Neckar.

In 1963, Mauser acquired the production rights to a sports rifle with a short bolt, developed by the renowned shooting and rifle dealer Walter Gehmann. This bolt action rifle was introduced in 1965 as the Mauser Model 66. During the 1960s, the Parabellum pistol was reintroduced, as were rifles produced in external factories under the Mauser name. In 1995-1996 the Mauser Company was taken over by the Rheinmetall Group. The gun-producing section of the company became Mauser-Werke Oberndorf Waffensysteme GmbH. At this time the Mauser Model 96 was introduced as the new hunting bolt action rifle with a straight pull action.

In 2000, Mauser Jagdwaffen GmbH and its European sister companies, J.P. Sauer & Sohn, Blaser and Swiss Arms, were unified by the German investors Michael Lüke and Thomas Ortmeier under the SIGARMS name.

2003 saw the introduction of the M03 hunting/sporting bolt-action rifle. This is a rifle with numerous innovations, the likes of which have not been seen at Mauser since the legendary Model 98 and the Model 66. The Mauser action was was originally designed for the military, but was soon adopted by sporting enthusiasts because of the reputation it gained as an infantry weapon. Many makers of quality custom rifles still use the Mauser action on which to build their own firearm.

The main feature of the M03 is its capacity to easily swap barrels and calibres. This is facilitated by the use of a full steel inner chassis that combines the receiver and barrel mounting bar in the forend; the barrel is secured by two fixed studs under the chamber, enabling the barrels to be quickly swapped by use of a torx key. The bolt has interchangeable heads that can be used on different calibre cartridges, while the magazine comes in one size but will accommodate a range of ammunition by using a packer filling internally.

The M03 has a large heavy bolt that does nothing to detract from the wholesome feel of this rifle, in fact, if anything, it has been engineered in a way and with such interesting features that it is a pure pleasure to use. The receiver allows easy access in the event of a jammed cartridge or for being single loaded if required. Because of its length it is able to take calibres from .222 up to .375.

The one-piece scope mount and scope must be removed before taking off the barrel, but the quick release design allows it to be taken off and replaced easily and without being detrimental to accuracy or causing a loss of zero.

The classically designed stock comes in a high quality walnut on the standard model and with a beautiful deeply grained

The Mauser M03 has the capacity to quickly and easily swap barrels and calibres

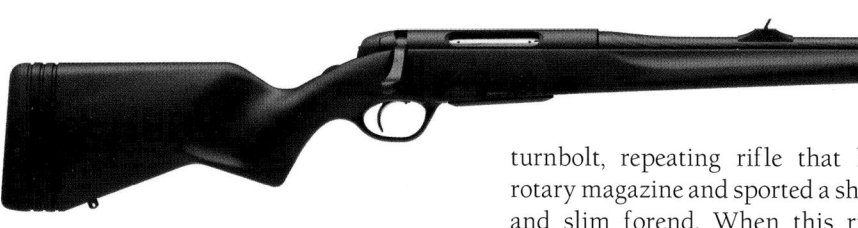

richly coloured variant on the deluxe version. Its style allows for ideal eye to optic alignment. The rifle comes in either a satin black, weather resistant, non-glare finish or a deluxe silver-nitrated finish along with a very pleasing piece of engraving.

I tested a .308 standard M03 and found it to be an absolute pleasure to use, partly due to the single-set trigger being crisp and not unduly heavy, and maybe also because of the robust feel when handling the weapon. Being very slightly on the heavy side at 7.75 pounds, recoil was, I felt, minimal.

At 100 yards using Norma 180-grain Nosler Partition rounds and an 8x56 Schmidt & Bender scope I was comfortably making one-inch groups. I feel this is a lot of rifle for the money, though remember the dedicated scope mounts cost extra.

The Steyr Mannlicher Pro Hunter
The Steyr arms factory was founded in the city of the same name in Austria back in 1864, and at first was responsible for the manufacture of military weapons. Not long after setting up production the company turned its attention to sporting rifles and so a legend was born. Two men were responsible for the most famous rifle that this company turned out: Ferdinand von Mannlicher and Otto Schoenauer, who were firearm designers. Mannlicher became famous for the many military actions that he designed, but it was Schoenauer's rotary magazine that became better known.

The name Mannlicher Schoenauer became synonymous with a stylish turnbolt, repeating rifle that housed a rotary magazine and sported a short barrel and slim forend. When this rifle went out of production in the late 1960s it was replaced by one of more modern design the now familiar Steyr Mannlicher.

The particular Steyr Prohunter rifle that I tested is owned by a friend of mine and is chambered for the 7mm Rem. Mag. It has a synthetic stock, a 25.6-inch rotary, cold hammer forged barrel, a detachable two-position magazine, a three-position rotary tang safety, a user adjustable trigger set at 3.5-4.0 lbs ex-factory, a silky smooth four-lug stainless steel bolt, is drilled and tapped to accept standard Browning A-bolt scope mounts, and has an adjustable length of pull by use of $1/4$-inch spacers. The overall length is 46.5 inches, and the catalogue weight is approximately 7.5 pounds. With a Kahles 10x42 scope, rings, and sling, his Steyr weighs a reasonable 8.75 pounds.

A little bit more should be said about the action on the Styer Prohunter, also known as the Styer Safebolt, which has to one of the most innovative rifle modernisations in recent years.

The revolutionary bolt action design of the Safe Bolt System (SBS) must represent the next generation of Steyr precision rifles, and should be a trendsetter for future bolt action rifles. The action, which is the focal point of the Steyr SBS, has a totally rigid, high strength, steel receiver which houses its unique Safe Bolt. Boasting four locking lugs, the SBS bolt is stronger than necessary, and has a rotation of only 60 degrees, which is all that is needed for it to be unlocked. Grooves in the bolt body guarantee reliable function under adverse conditions, and the bolt field strips in seconds without tools. Testing has been carried out to safeguard against

The Steyr Mannlicher Pro Hunter features the revolutionary Safe Bolt System

unexpected excessive chamber pressures up to 120,000 psi. Conventional proofing is carried out with loads that produce only up to 70,000 psi. Steyr's high quality cold hammer forged match grade barrel is screwed into the receiver. As I have already said the SBS's smooth trigger is adjustable, and of the two-stage military type; it comes set at just over three pounds from the factory. Even with the safety in the 'fire' position, no amount of slamming the butt on the floor will make the SBS fire. The receiver is a closed top design, and this makes it difficult to manually load a cartridge into the chamber through the ejection port.

Where people are concerned, no mechanical device is 100 per cent safe, and firearm safety is something that we all need to take seriously; ultimately safety is the responsibility of anyone who handles a weapon. However, Steyr has incorporated safety design features into the SBS that dramatically improve safe handling and usage. The SBS roller tang safety has three positions: fire, load/unload and safe. The logic cannot be faulted; when the safety is forward, bullets can go forward (fire), and when rolled back bullets stay back (safe). In the middle (loading position), rounds can be loaded or removed from the chamber, but the SBS cannot fire.

In this rear position a white dot is visible; the rifle cannot be fired and the bolt is locked, but this is only part of the safety feature. As an added measure of caution, the bolt handle may also be pushed down about an eighth of an inch to the double lock-safe position, where the firing pin is shifted out of alignment. When the safety catch is moved to off safe, the bolt handle moves back up to its normal position.

The stock on the rifle that I used is a synthetic composite type and comes with removable butt-plate spacers that can be used to adjust the length of pull. It is adjustable from approximately 12.75 inches to 13.75 inches. The stock is ergonomically designed, with a flat bottomed forend that rests naturally on a branch or shooting rail. Although it is synthetic, the stock feels very natural and seems to focus the recoil down and away from the face. It fits the rear hand nicely, and has a slight palm swell.

The Steyer Mannlicher SBS Prohunter comes in a variety of versions and calibres including .243 Win., 25/06, .270 Win., 6.5x55, 7x64, 7mm/08, .308 Win., .30/06, 7mm Rem. Mag., .300 Win. Mag, 8x57JS and 9.3x62.

Using Hornady's 7mm Heavy Magnum factory loaded 139-grain cartridges I managed to shoot some tight groups. Although some of the shots in the three-round volleys I fired went wide, the average group was within a 1.25-inch circle.

This is an excellent hunting rifle that has many desirable engineering features, including the two position magazine, adjustable length of pull, easy to use rotary tang safety, and Millet flush mount swing swivels. It has a high degree of intrinsic accuracy and a superior quality, rotary cold hammer forged barrel. I have collected the old Mannlicher Schoenauers for many years, but I think that the Steyer Mannlicher SBS Pro Hunter is a good reason for me to upgrade into the 21st century.

The Sako 85 Hunter

The name Sako is an acronym for Suojeluskuntain Ase-ja Konepaja Oy (Civil Guard Gun and Machine Works Ltd) and is a Finnish firearm manufacturer formed in 1927. Since then a few organisational changes have taken place, and in 1987 the state owned company Valmet and Sako merged to form Sako-Valmet, with 50 per cent of the company being owned by Nokia. After more organisational shifts in the year 2000, Beretta made a substantial investment in Sako and they now effectively control the company.

The Sako name is associated with quality, accuracy and yet reasonably priced products. Tikka rifles are a lower priced option also made by the Sako Company.

The Sako 85 Hunter rifle has a number of actions and are designated as: Extra Short, also known as XS; Short, or S; and Short Magnum, or SM. There is also a Medium action and a Long action, also known as M and L respectively. The actions offer traditional Sako features, such as action sizes matched to cartridges, mechanical ejection and an integral tapered scope mount rail. Additionally, on the Model 85 there is a controlled feed mechanism in order to ensure reliable cartridge feed to the chamber. The magazine is detachable and the rifle can also be directly loaded through the ejection port.

The single-stage trigger pull is adjustable from two to four pounds, and a single-set trigger is available as an additional option. The safety catch has a mechanism that allows loading and unloading of the rifle with safety engaged. The oil-finished walnut stock is of classic design with a strong, extended recoil lug incorporated in the forend. The open sights with a post bead are adjustable for windage and elevation, while integral rails for the scope mounts are fitted to the receiver.

The Sako 85 action includes a front locking bolt with three lugs that cocks on opening. The bolt lugs are integral with the bolt body and rotation is through 70 degrees. The biggest change in the 85 action compared to its predecessor the Model 75 is what Sako advertise as 'controlled cartridge feeding'.

The receiver is of a machined steel, flat bottomed design and, as already mentioned, the ejection port is well enough proportioned to allow cartridges to be single loaded directly into the chamber; a desirable feature on a hunting rifle.

The back of the bolt is shrouded, and an extension at the end of the striker bearing a red dot protrudes from beneath this shroud when the striker is cocked. The bolt release is located at the left rear of the action and pressing the rear of the release simply and easily removes the bolt.

When you have removed the bolt it is important not to turn the shroud unless you intend to disassemble it. Just a slight rotation of the shroud and the bolt tends to spring apart, and unfortunately it comes apart far more easily than it goes back together. However, when you want to take the bolt apart for cleaning, it is certainly easy to do without the use of tools.

The safety catch is a two position slider, which is put in the forward position for fire and is located at the right and to the rear of the receiver, just behind the bolt handle. In its rearward position the safety locks the bolt closed, but this feature can be overridden by depressing

The Sako 85 is available in a number of actions

Chapter 4 — HUNTING WILD BOAR IN BRITAIN: THE EQUIPMENT

a small metal button immediately in front of the safety. Pressing this button allows the bolt to be operated with the safety on; a good system that sounds a bit odd, but works very well and may help prevent accidental bolt opening caused by snagging in the field.

The extractor is a claw mounted at the front of the bolt, while the ejector is located at the rear of the receiver and is spring loaded. The rate at which the bolt is pulled back determines how forcefully the case is ejected, in the same way as the Mauser 98 type fixed ejector. Both the extractor and ejector work well.

The Sako 85 feeds cartridges from a removable, staggered row, sheet metal box magazine with what appears to be an aluminium follower. The magazine latch is in front of the flush fitting magazine and must be pushed to the back to release the magazine. Removing the magazine requires that latch is pushed back at the same time that the magazine is pushed up into the rifle, making the process slightly irritating. Failure to push the magazine up renders the latch immoveable. On the positive side however, once the magazine is released and removed from the rifle, loading it is very easy, as is loading it the through the ejection port with the magazine in situ.

I am not sure that the controlled feed action works particularly well on the Sako 85. The extractor is much smaller than the full length extractors on a Mauser 98, and takes a smaller bite on the case rim. If you close the Sako's bolt about halfway until you hear the next cartridge in the magazine click up, and then pull the bolt back and try to close it again, it will jam the rifle by attempting to double feed. In that situation, a controlled feed action should hold onto the first cartridge until the bolt is completely withdrawn and it is ejected. If the bolt is run forward again while still holding the first cartridge, the extractor should keep it in place and guide it into the chamber, thus preventing the bolt from attempting to pick-up the second cartridge and thereby preventing a jam. The Sako's extractor only seems to take a strong hold on the cartridge at the very end of its journey to the chamber, by which time it's a bit late.

On the plus side, the Sako's extractor will easily over-ride the rim of a cartridge fed directly into the chamber, like any other push feed action, and its receiver mounted ejector lets a reloader deposit fired brass neatly to hand by opening the bolt slowly.

However the most important thing is that most users will appreciate the Sako 85 operates smoothly and feeds reliably. Its action is noticeably smoother than some other rifles of its class, although in my opinion it is not quite as smooth as a Steyr Mannlicher or a Mauser M03. All of these are good rifles, it just shows that there is no such thing as a perfect hunting rifle; each design has its strengths and weaknesses.

The hammer-forged, free-floating barrel sports a target type crown, in fact Sako make a feature of this in their promotional material, however I believe that this may well be more susceptible to damage in the field.

Sako rifles come with a 100 yard, one-inch accuracy guarantee, and I am pleased to say that when I took mine to the range, I was able to do just that. There are of course many other rifles that can do that straight out of the box, but I don't believe there are many other manufacturers who guarantee it. I am sure that there are many riflemen out there who would never achieve these results no matter what rifle or ammunition they use, so I don't quite know how Sako get around that.

I was using a Model 85 Hunter chambered in .243 Win fed Federal 100-grain Nosler Partition ammunition and with a 4-12x50 Swarovski scope on top. This is an ideal combination for roe deer and muntjac, the latter of which might adequately be taken with the smaller 80-grain bullet; as indeed could ground game and vermin.

The walnut stock on my test rifle had attractive grain with ample fine line

There is no perfect rifle and scope combo for boar, and much of the choice is down to personal preference

checkering at the forend and pistol grip. The stock finish is a matt lacquer and the butt was finished with a solid black rubber pad, with detachable sling swivel studs provided. This stock looked attractive and well-shaped, but at the same time was robust in appearance. I would say that the price is on the high end for an off-the-shelf production rifle.

Browning X-Bolt
John Browning was one of 22 children; his father, Jonathan, being a good Mormon, had three wives. Gun-making ran in the family and just before his father died he handed the family business over to his son John who despite being desperately short of funds and having no experience with machine tools, transformed the small gun store into a thriving workshop employing seven people.

John and his brother Matt had struggled in the early years, but eventually one of their inventions caught the eye of the managing director of Winchester who travelled to what was, at the time, 'the wild west' in order to meet the brothers.

A deal was struck between Winchester and the Browning brothers that lasted for several decades. John Browning granted licenses to several manufacturers over the years allowing them to use his inventions and make his firearms.

In 1897 the Belgium Company Fabrique Nationale obtained a license to produce the 7.65 Browning pistol that incorporated a novel locking mechanism, and so began an uninterrupted alliance between the arms factory in Belgium and the Mormon inventor from Utah. The peak of John Browning's personal inventiveness was in designing the Auto-5, semi automatic shotgun which was a tremendous commercial success and prompted his first visit to the FN Factory in Herstal, Belgium. He died in 1926 on his g1st visit to the factory of a heart attack. His body was taken back to the US for burial with full military honours.

The Browning X-Bolt rifle was introduced in 2008 and I noticed it created a lot of interest at the Safari Club International's Annual convention in Reno soon after. With that in mind I was more than happy to get the opportunity to test fire it. I picked up The Hunter model, which came with a walnut stock wearing a synthetic satin finish, while its barrel and action had a low-lustre blue finish. This new rifle has a bolt action push feed that cocks on opening and uses a new, detachable magazine system.

At the Browning booth in Reno last year I had a long conversation with a Browning representative who showed me the new X-Bolt rifle with considerable pride, pointing out the new action's advantages, and explaining its features. In the course of that conversation, an interested onlooker, not being shy about such things, pointed out the drawbacks of a detachable magazine in a hunting rifle and I was surprised when the Browning representative agreed with him. He readily admitted that, like the new interested party, he preferred an internal box magazine with a hinged floorplate, but told us that the sales department had demanded a detachable magazine because that is the current fad.

As detachable magazine systems go, the X-Bolt's is extremely good, possibly one of the best that I have ever used in fact. The magazine body is made of a high-impact polymer, which is less likely to be damaged in use than a steel magazine. Polymer magazines also seem to feed more smoothly than steel magazines. This one holds four rounds in a sort of rotary system that feeds cartridges into the chamber in a straight line and is exceptionally easy to load. The magazine fits easily into the rifle and it doesn't matter if you stick the front or the back of the magazine in first, or insert it level it just clicks securely into place.

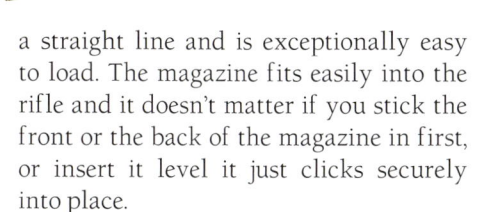

The magazine feed is reliable and the rifle can be single loaded by inserting a cartridge directly into the chamber or by simply dropping a cartridge into the loading port on top of the empty magazine and closing the bolt. It is a very reliable push feed action. The one-piece bottom iron and trigger guard is made from an alloy and its finish is a perfect match for the matt blue action. The trigger guard bow itself has a squared shape at the front and it allows adequate space for gloved fingers. The steel X-Bolt receiver has three wide facets on top that are more or less the same shape of the bolt body it contains. It uses a separate recoil lug fitted between the barrel and receiver. A convenient bolt release is located at the left rear of the receiver, which is pressed in to remove the bolt. The top of the receiver is drilled and tapped to accept X-Bolt scope bases.

The bolt assembly uses a steel bolt body, a separate bolt head double pinned into place at the front, a bolt handle assembly on a collar that is pinned in place at the rear and a shroud that is pinned in place at the very back. The bolt head uses three locking lugs at the front of the bolt, which ride in grooves in the receiver as the bolt is withdrawn to minimise slop; it requires only a 60 degree bolt rotation to open or close. When the bolt is pulled all the way back, wobble is noticeably less than with a conventional Mauser 98-type action.

The A-Bolt's familiar bolt shroud and rotating bolt head are gone. The whole X-Bolt rotates when the handle is lifted, as per conventional bolt action. The body is polished and left in the white and the blued bolt handle terminates in the very distinct, angled and flattened ball made popular by the A-Bolt, which is arguably the best shaped and most comfortable bolt knob on the market. The X-Bolt extractor is a small Sako type at the front of the recessed bolt face and the ejector is of the plunger type. The shroud, which appears to be made of aluminium and is pinned in place at the rear of the bolt, is streamlined and designed to keep powder gasses from a blown primer or a ruptured case out of the shooter's face.

The new trigger was set at the factory with about a four-pound pull, which was very clean and without creep. I understand that to adjust the pull weight is a very simple procedure that just entails removing the stock, by undoing two bolts, and turning the trigger adjustment screw to its optimum position. As conventional

The Browning X-Bolt with its removable magazine

Chapter 4 — HUNTING WILD BOAR IN BRITAIN: THE EQUIPMENT

(non-AccuTrigger) hunting rifle triggers go today, this is about as good as it gets.

The two-position, tang mounted safety is smooth, positive and quiet in operation. It locks the bolt closed when applied. The slider's rear position is safe and forward is fire. An unusual feature is a small, square button at the root of the bolt handle that pops up when the safety is switched on. Depressing this allows the bolt to be opened with the safety on to remove an unfired cartridge from the chamber.

The barrelled action is glass bedded in the stock. The X-Bolt's barrel is free floating and the muzzle is finished with a target crown. It seems that this is another manufacturer's trend currently to put target crowns on hunting rifles, but I don't understand why.

The X-Bolt Hunter stock differs considerably from the previous, A-Bolt Hunter stock and has no cap on the pistol grip, which has slight palm swelling for comfort. The comb is deeply fluted and high enough to position the eye correctly behind a telescopic sight. The forend incorporates a wide, downward slanting finger groove that seemingly serves no practical purpose except to reduce the forend's checkering coverage, and therefore presumably making it slightly cheaper to produce. Browning should be congratulated for using genuine hand checkering on this medium priced rifle. The checkering patterns on both the pistol grip and the forend do not in my opinion blend very well with the outline of the stock.

The bottom iron for the new detachable box magazine system extends laterally all the way across the bottom of the stock and well up both sides, an unusual arrangement. The barrel is free floated in the forend channel and overall the inletting of the barrelled action into the stock was about average for today's factory built rifles.

The butt terminates in a very soft, rounded and contoured, one-inch thick recoil pad. Detachable sling swivels are provided. Aesthetically, this new stock leaves something to be desired. Mostly, it needs to be cleaned-up and made more elegant.

The weight, balance and overall handling of the basic X-Bolt Hunter are good and there is always the Medallion version if you want a fancier upgrade. The Medallion is functionally identical to the Hunter, but features upgraded wood with a rosewood forend tip and pistol grip cap, glossy stock finish and a high-polished, lustre blued barrelled action.

The X-Bolt Hunter that I tried was fitted with a Schmidt & Bender, Zenith 1.1-4x24 scope along with the impressive Flash dot reticle. This I felt would be an ideal scope for hunting in Africa although maybe not first choice for deer stalking in Scotland.

On the range when I tested this rifle I used Federal Low Recoil 170-grain FP ammunition, which I was firing at 100 yards. In three-shot bursts the smallest group I managed was one inch and the largest half an inch bigger.

Ruger Hawkeye

Bill Ruger is a well known modern gun designer whose achievements include, among others, the single-shot No.1 lever action carbine, the Mini 14 and a whole range of handguns. All are or were successful and manufactured in large numbers from the company he founded, Sturm Ruger & Co in Southport, Connecticut. The most popular rifle that his company produced is the highly modernised Mauser-type, turnbolt centrefire, known as the M77. The original M77 was introduced in 1968 and came in only one grade, but with a choice of a number of popular calibres. The Hawkeye is the latest addition to the M77 design.

I tested this rifle along with others, which perhaps led me to feel slightly disappointed with its performance. Had I tried it in isolation I may have rated the Ruger Hawkeye a very good rifle. I didn't though, and it suffered by the comparison. This illustrates the value of comparative testing rather than simply trying a weapon on its own.

For example, this M77 Hawkeye is fitted with Ruger's new LC6 trigger (standing for "light and crisp"). It is not a bad trigger and it has no obvious take-up, so I can happily agree with the crisp description. However it was one of the heaviest triggers tested, with a pull weight of about four pounds 11 ounces. The LC6 is not terrible, but in my opinion is too heavy for rifle to be used for stalking or for that matter ground vermin.

Aesthetically the Ruger is pleasing and the stock had the best grade of walnut that you could expect of a rifle in its price range. It had a wonderful distinctive grain and the red rubber butt pad looked stylish. I am unsure about the Ruger's matt blue metal finish, though; it is nicely done, but the maker's standard polished blue has generally been excellent and in my opinion is more attractive.

The action is the well-known KM77 MKII variant. This is an investment cast, controlled feed action with a nicely turned bolt handle for good scope clearance. The Ruger Hawkeye was mounted with a 2-12x50mm Swarovski Z6I scope using the medium rings supplied by Ruger. These rings inspired confidence and I appreciated that the rings come with hex head caps, not the old flat blade screwdriver slots that were previously a bit of a hassle.

The Hawkeye has an internal, staggered cartridge, steel box magazine similar to the Mauser 98 with a hinged floor plate. The floor plate release and trigger guard are very nicely done. There is no attempt to free-float the barrel; it maintains essentially full wood contact all the way from the tip of the forend to the action.

At first when I cast my eye over this rifle, the nice wood and integral rings that were supplied by the manufacturer are easy to work with, I thought that the Ruger was well on its way to winning the comparison. However when I started shooting it quickly become obvious that

The Ruger Hawkeye with its trigger unit inset

the Hawkeye is sluggishly heavy with a trigger that I felt less than comfortable using. I did not feel that it was top of the league in the accuracy department, making on average 21/8 inch groups at 100 yards; I was using .270 Winchester, 100-grain Super X ammunition. While I was more than pleased with these results, I did get slightly tighter groups with other rifles that I tested.

At the end of the day, despite the Ruger's strong action, attention to build detail and nice wood, I decided that I personally could do better with the other brands.

The Chapuis

The most iconic of all hunting weapons surely must be the double rifle. It probably is to the hunter what the AK47 is to the mercenary – a must have firearm. I wonder, though, if the magic of a double rifle is in the image it conjures up of the intrepid hunter on safari under the African sun with his rifle slung over his shoulder in a cavalier fashion, looking for all the world like Stewart Granger in *King Solomon's Mines* or Robert Redford in *Out of Africa*.

Ever since reading such great authors as Ernest Hemingway and Peter Hathaway Capstick, or learning of the exploits of Frederick Courteney Selous and Denys Finch Hatton, I had longed to own my own double rifle. Of course like many before me I dreamed of an English double, and I imagined that I would be using it in Africa, but, like so many things in life, reality dictated otherwise.

I looked at what English guns were available at a price that I could afford and learned that there were precisely none. That is, there were plenty of English double rifles that were for sale, but none that I could afford. When I did eventually buy my first double rifle some years later it came from an unexpected source, it was not English and it was not for use in Africa.

A good friend of mine had hit on hard times and wanted to sell his unused Chapuis RGEX Ejector double rifle chambered for 9.3x74R. It just so happened that at that time I was due to go on a wild boar hunt in France and could hardly believe how fitting it would be take my new weapon back to its country of origin with me. The 9.3x74R is of course a classic European round for wild boar. It's not English, but then neither was the price. What it was, however, was an awful lot of gun for the money, and I had a great time using it.

Chapuis Armes was founded in the 1920s by Jean Chapuis, the father of the current owner Rene. The company relocated in the late 1980s into a brand new factory that boasts an underground 100-metre range, as well as integrating all of its workshops under one roof.

One of the advantages of using a double rifle is the ability to fire two shots in rapid succession without the need to change position in the slightest and without the risk of jamming. Every experienced hunter knows how important this can be especially when chasing dangerous game.

The RGEX is a boxlock design and comes with blued 22.5-inch barrels with double under lugs that are hand regulated in the traditional manner. Among its many features, it sports a pistol grip complete with a steel cap, a walnut butt plate and a non-automatic safety. The barrels are factory regulated with 285-grain Norma Oryx factory load, plus it has all the niceties such as ejectors, double triggers and a long tang trigger guard that you might expect from a quality double rifle.

The stock is made from a beautiful block of hand rubbed, oil finished, quality Turkish walnut with a classic English style cheek piece, finished with hand cut checkering on the pistol grip and a beavertail forend.

It was here in fact where I parted company with the manufacturer's choice of design. Beavertail forends are clumsy and dumpy looking at the best of times and should never, in my opinion, be used on a double rifle. The idea is that they stop the shooters hand slipping forward and coming in contact with the hot barrels. This is all well and good on a shotgun that may be fired multiple times on a driven pheasant shoot, but not so with a big game gun. The proper technique used for double rifles, is to wrap the fingers over the barrel. It's not such an issue on this little rifle, but step up to something like a 577NE and the beavertail starts to get in the way a little.

Another small bone of contention, for me anyway, was that I felt that the comb was a bit too high. This seems to be a common issue with off-the-shelf doubles built for mass consumption, in other words not built to the customer's personal specification. The problem could be largely solved by fitting a scope on quickly detachable swivel mounts; however I resisted doing this as I wanted to retain the elegance of the weapon and use open sights.

Attention has been paid to the engraving, which is a combination of game scenes, and of course I particularly like the intricate detail on the image of a wild boar, and floral patterns.

The rifle weighs just a tad over six pounds making it nice and light to carry, but at only six pounds, and chambered for the powerful 9.3x74R cartridge, the recoil does grab your attention. When the Chapuis is fired you do not only hear it with your ears, but the sound seems to travel throughout your entire body. It is not just heard, the blast is felt as the sharp recoil abuses not only your shoulder, but your entire being. The recoil velocity in particular is high, and for that reason I limited my time on the range to about 15 minutes in order to avoid developing a flinch. However as with other big calibre weapons that I have used, all of the above becomes similar to using a rimfire rifle when shooting game; the adrenalin released in the heat of the moment on a real hunt seems to divert all attention away from any discomfort that may be felt.

The pull on the triggers of my Chapuis were set at between 4.25 and 4.75 pounds and I was never aware of any creep. The sights were nice and easy to use, although I think I would have preferred a two or three leaf express sight on the rear and a simple gold bead on the front. Not only would this have looked more traditional, I think it would have made the rifle slightly more versatile.

On the range I was shooting Norma 285-grain plastic point, and although in other large calibre bolt action rifles this ammunition gives me good tight patterns, I was not able to achieve the same results at 100 yards with my Chapuis.

After putting 100 rounds down, I decided that this particular double rifle is a charge stopper or for close range work. At 50 yards I was getting average groups of about three inches. At 100 yards I found that it was difficult to consistently make acceptable groups. As I have already mentioned, the rifle had been regulated with 285-grain Norma Oryx loads and so I intend to try the rifle out again using that ammunition to see if that makes a difference.

In conclusion I would have to say that I was highly impressed by the appearance and the way in which the RGEX handles. In general terms the double rifle's strength is in its quick handling ability and the speed of the second shot. Conversely, however, its most talked about weakness is (apart from price) its lack of accuracy. My experience with my Chapuis leads me to the very same conclusion.

HUNTING WILD BOAR IN BRITAIN: THE EVENT

Having acquired the necessary information to embark on a wild boar hunt, all that is left is to get out in the field and try your luck. You have a good knowledge of the creature's habits, appearance and numbers, and careful consideration has been given to the calibre and make of rifle, as well as the type of optics you will use on the weapon.

Once you've decided whether you'll be sitting in a hide or shooting on the move, all that remains is to take the shot. Yet there is one question left to consider: which animal do you shoot and which do you leave?

The answer lies very much in the outcome that is wanted by you, the hunter, or possibly with the landowner on whose land the wild boars are to be pursued. As I have already mentioned, in the UK wild boar tend to be regarded as vermin by the authorities rather than a worthy game animal that was once indigenous to Britain. Therefore, in my opinion, they should have the protection in law and closed hunting seasons that deer enjoy. Sadly, however, this is not the case. Therefore if your goal is eradication rather than controlled management, just keep plenty of lead in the air until they are all gone.

On the other hand, good management will depend on several criteria. Although ultimately, maintaining overall numbers to within parameters that allow the boar to live harmoniously with farmers and other folk in the area will provide the main incentive.

How many do you shoot?

This will depend on how many there are to start with, and how much damage is being caused by rooting up crops or valuable pasture land. Clearly a forest terrain in Scotland will sustain far less damage than an arable piece of farmland in Sussex. On the contrary to causing damage, some researchers have shown that wild boar will actually improve a woodland ecology and diversity through their rooting activity. Not all the evidence is positive in this regard, but it stands to reason that the damage caused will be less in certain areas than in others.

Without doubt the way to manage numbers will be to cull females. The question that then always arises is should pregnant females or sows with piglets at foot be killed?

A good boar management strategy will allow boar and humans to live harmoniously

WILD BOAR – A BRITISH PERSPECTIVE

Chapter 5 — HUNTING WILD BOAR IN BRITAIN: THE EVENT

It is likely that any mature female that is not accompanied by youngsters will be pregnant, and so trying to determine whether a sow is in pig or not will be a fruitless exercise. If the population needs to be kept in check then all unaccompanied females will be fair game.

In a management cull, females with dependant youngsters at foot should be left alone and the only justification in shooting her is if the total eradication of wild boar in the area is demanded, in which case, after killing the mother, every attempt to kill her dependants should be made.

In order to maintain the integrity of a sounder during a management cull, it is a good policy not to shoot the matriarch or dominant sow, sometimes known as the *laie meneuse*, if she can be easily identified. This sow is experienced in finding the herd food, leading them to safety, finding wallows and waterholes and generally looking after their wellbeing. It would seem that she is able to memorise game paths, safe refuges and secluded spots to lie up in during the day. Her early demise will therefore lead to chaos within the group unless there is an experienced second in command ready to take her place. The mature sow is also a good breeder, producing larger litters than her younger counterparts, which, in a well-managed herd being preserved for sporting purposes or even meat production, is all important. Again it really comes down to whether the animals in question are considered pests or assets.

These older matriarchs are also good teachers, and it will be necessary to conserve a fairly high percentage of this female age group in order to maintain a truly free ranging self-sufficient sounder, where its younger members have been taught how to fend for themselves.

An advantage of concentrating on the younger females in the group when culling is of course the excellent meat that is harvested. Unlike the wild boar's cousin, the domestic pig, wild boar produce a red meat and is of a totally different taste and texture to pork.

Young males are forced to leave the sounder when they become sexually mature at about 10 months to a year. They will then form small bachelor herds or sometimes even mixed herds with females that have been pushed out of their group because the numbers in their original family are too great. Curiously, although understandably, the age at which the male is sexually mature is dependent upon the size of his testicles, which need to be in the order of two ounces in weight. Regrettably for the young boar, this also makes him eligible for the pot, and as many 50 per cent of this age of males would be candidates in a management cull.

Distinguishing between young boars and young sows is not always so easy, especially in the heat of the moment when the adrenalin is surging through your blood vessels, triggered by the appearance of the quarry you have been waiting for all afternoon and evening. The difficulty is made worse as light fades and much of the detail of what you are looking at is lost. However this does not signal the end of play, because both young females and young boars are fair game. Although the youngsters are similar in appearance to each other, the differences between males and females and juveniles and adults become clearer as they get older. As both boars and sows grow into mature middle age they lose the square shape of the juvenile and begin to bulk out and grow taller. The sow will get bigger and taller, but in an ill-defined way she will still retain some of her more, for want of a better word, delicate features.

The boar on the other hand begins to develop a much heavier front end. As the balance of his weight shifts forward his shoulders gain height as well as bulk, making the line of his back slope down to his haunches. His body becomes more muscular and the thick coarse hair that covers his entire body becomes even thicker around the shoulders and head, giving him a vaguely similar profile, albeit in miniature, to a bison. As the boar gets older his tusks become longer and sharper and his body continues to develop in the manner just described. He becomes more solitary, only seeking female company as the sow comes into oestrus.

This is the trophy hunters dream – a truly big keiler! The mature keiler is certainly not a cull animal, and if he has shown the necessary guile to grow old and become such a magnificent beast, it would certainly be advantageous to allow him to pass on some of his genes to the next generation. That said, there will not be too many opportunities to take a really mature boar like this, especially in the UK, but when it happens it is truly memorable. In summary, once you have an idea of the number of wild boar living in the area you will then be able to estimate by how much you want to reduce that number. The figure you are left with will be the total number of animals to be killed and should be taken in the following ratio. 70 per cent juveniles, 20 per cent middle aged, 10 per cent old animals (either trophies or infirm).

In some ways, when culling it is useful to think of yourself as if you were a natural predator of the species that you

The author (right) and Byron Pace with a keiler shot on the Shooting Show

Chapter 5 — HUNTING WILD BOAR IN BRITAIN: THE EVENT

The most common shot placements for wild boar are ringed, though the safest, in the author's opinion, is always the heart shot

are hunting. It is likely that by far the largest number of prey taken by a natural predator will be youngsters and old, infirm individuals. As we are managing these numbers by what is unnatural means, we can manipulate these figures to our advantage.

SHOT PLACEMENT

So you have chosen your gun, which is chambered for the calibre that you have decided will work best for you, and it is mounted with a scope that is the best you can afford. You have been sitting in your hide for some time and finally an ideal beast comes into range. Where are you going to place your shot for a clean, humane kill?

There are three vital areas that will drop your animal instantly, but only one can really be recommended and that is a heart shot. The other two are the brain and the cervical spine.

The brain shot should not be attempted by beginners... or experienced riflemen either. The brain is relatively small and sits in a skull made of thick bone. It is all so easy for a bullet to deflect off the skull if the angle at which it is shot is not correct. It is even easier to blow the jaw off the unfortunate animal and condemn it to a slow and agonising death.

A neck shot is occasionally acceptable, but should only be attempted by an experienced shot that has a good knowledge of the anatomy of wild boar. As you would have seen from simply looking at pictures of these animals, *Sus scrofa* is not known for the length of its neck, and especially when in full winter coat the neck is very ill-defined.

The other difficulty is finding the location of the vertebrae, which is not along the dorsal line of the body as might be expected. If the neck were to be likened

92 WILD BOAR – A BRITISH PERSPECTIVE

to a cylinder then the cervical vertebrae would be like a central core running along its axis.

The better aim point by far is the heart, which is located ventrally in the rib cage and approximately between the front legs. The trick here is to place the shot at the aim point, which is best located when the animal is sideways on, and then wait until it puts its nearest front leg forward, creating a triangle of lighter coloured hair between the body and leg.

Deer stalkers will recognise this as a method of locating the aim point on their quarry, but remember that the wild boar is a shorter animal than deer, and if the shot is being taken from a high seat then it will be a markedly downhill target. If anything, take the shot slightly high, but still forward of the diaphragm because the heart lies very low in the chest cavity and a low shot may just incur a flesh wound. If the shot is just a few inches high it will cause fatal damage to the lungs and major pulmonary blood vessels; a good lung shot will not allow the animal go far and is likely to leave a prolific blood trail that is easy to follow.

Immediately after the shot, reload and watch what happens next. If the animal had no idea that you were there then a good shot will lay him flat where he stood. Sometimes a boar may know that there is somebody close by and be very wary with adrenalin flowing in his bloodstream. In this case even a well-placed bullet may make him run further than might otherwise be expected. Depending on circumstances it may be wise to put a second insurance round into him, or watch and, if possible, see where he eventually falls. Clearly this may not be possible in thick cover, but at least you will be able to take note of the general direction in which he ran.

After the shot

Always give a fallen animal several minutes before approaching him and then do it with caution and ideally from uphill. A wounded wild boar can be an extremely dangerous adversary, especially if he is a big keiler. Ideally, if he is not dead, but unable to get to his feet, he should be despatched by putting another round into him as quickly as possible. High powered rifles are not always the best tool for that particular job especially if the animal has fallen on rocky terrain because of the risk of a ricochet. They are also a bit cumbersome if you have to get into a tight piece of cover. On more than one occasion I have had to crawl on hands and knees under sitka spruce trees or into rocky outcrops in order to finish off a wounded pig. In these circumstances a captive bolt or a handgun should be used for humane destruct. This is far safer than trying to do the same job with a knife, which I suggest would be highly irresponsible.

If the beast has been wounded, but is able to run off, then immediate action is needed, which may involve the use of tracker dogs, although some careful thought needs to go into this before using a dog that is not used to working with wild boar. As I have already said, these animals can be very dangerous and many a hound has been lost to due to an encounter with a wounded boar. On the other hand, if an experienced dog and handler are available then they can be invaluable in bringing the pig to bay while the *coup de grâce* is administered. Hounds are not used in the UK for hunting wild boar, but a good dog on a blood scent can save a lot of time searching for an animal that is very good at going to earth. Whichever way the animal is finally killed, the next step is to bleed it, and this should be done as a matter of some urgency. It is best done by getting the animal so that its head is facing downhill. Then insert a knife

Chapter 5 HUNTING WILD BOAR IN BRITAIN: THE EVENT

Shot wild boar should be taken back to the larder as soon as possible

Whenever possible, if I think that I will not be able to get back to base quickly, I like to use a mobile larder. This means that once the animal has been bled and eviscerated there is no hurry to carry out the rest of the meat or trophy preparation.

The gralloch

Whether you skin the animal first or eviscerate it is not too important, but there are one or two points to consider before you start. First of all if the carcase is going to a game dealer it must have the skin left on. Alternatively, it's probably a lot cleaner to remove the skin from the animal before opening up the body cavity, but this method should only be used if the carcase preparation is to be carried out immediately after bleeding in order that the meat is able cool down more rapidly. Even then it would be best done back at the larder. Usually this will not be convenient unless the hunting ground is close to your base. Under normal circumstances the animal will be killed, bled and the gut removed in the field.

It is best to start by removing all four of the lower legs at the joints while the animal is still on the ground. This is because the relatively short, stocky legs of the boar can resist the joint being broken once the ligament has been cut and it may require you to use your knee as a pivot to lever it against. If you are able to hang the carcase from a convenient tree then make a small slit with your knife just above the joint that has just been removed and between the bone and the ligament of the back legs. A gambrel can then be put in place and the carcase hauled up to a convenient height to work on.

Hold the penis in one hand and cut around it, then up to and around the scrotum. Remove the testicles along with the penis and, without cutting them off, lay them up and over the haunches to hang alongside

at the base of the neck, but just above the clavicle where it meets the sternum. The knife should point down towards the heart with the blade facing the dorsal aspect of the carcase, then simply sever the aorta. When done properly blood will gush out of the incision. It should then be taken back to the larder as soon as you are able, otherwise gralloch it on the spot in order to be able to open the carcase and let it cool down. This is absolutely essential in order to prevent the meat from going 'green' and thereby rendering it unfit for human consumption.

WILD BOAR – A BRITISH PERSPECTIVE

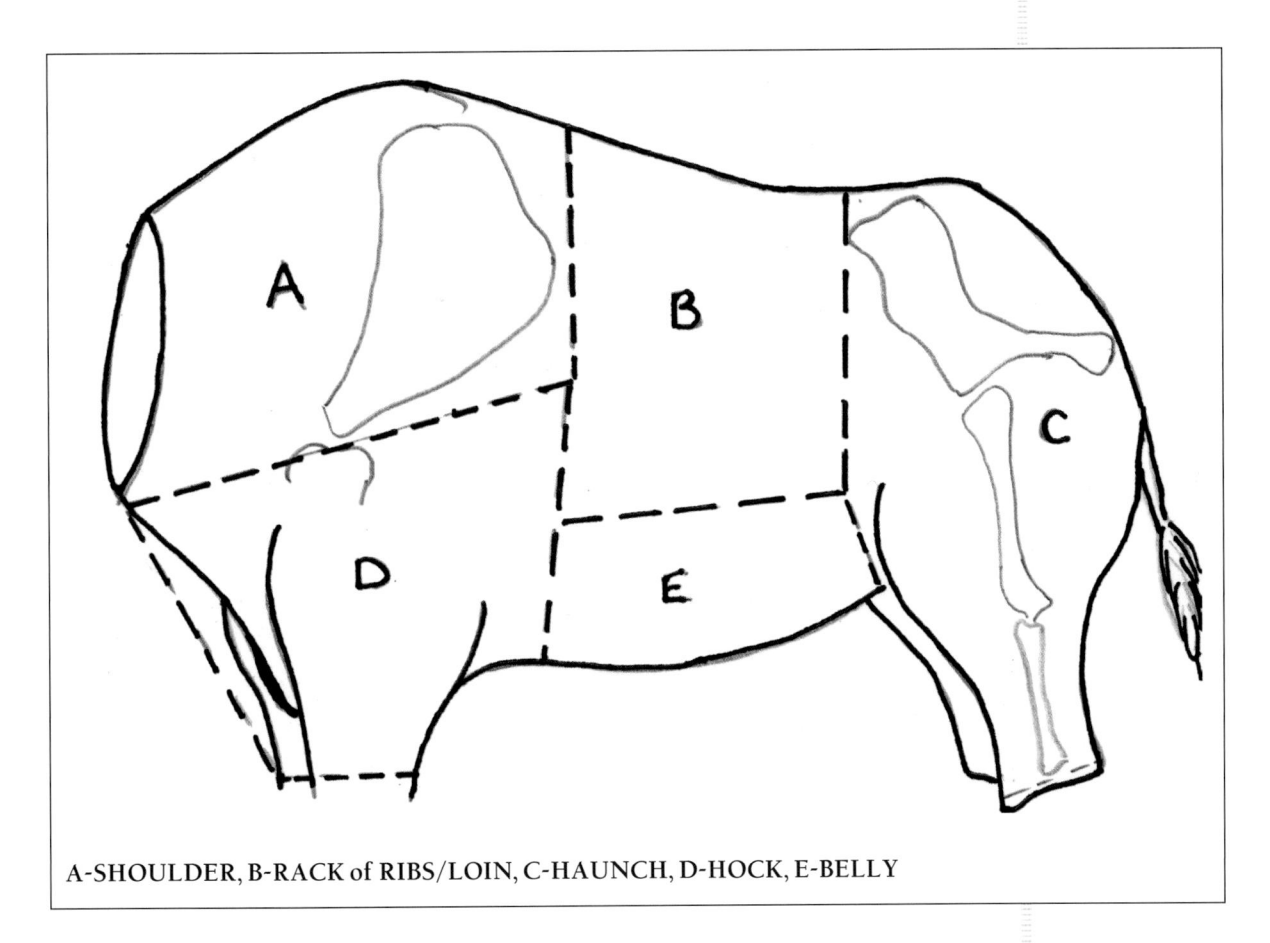

A-SHOULDER, B-RACK of RIBS/LOIN, C-HAUNCH, D-HOCK, E-BELLY

the tail. Excise the vas deferens and urethra along with any blood vessels away from the muscle tissue then cut the flesh down to the pelvis. It is now possible to cut around the anus and free the rectum. It is likely that the rectum and the intestines will be full, and so at this point it might be prudent to tie off the rectum with a ligature in order to prevent spillage and contamination.

Now using your forefinger and middle finger tease the skin and connective tissue away from the underlying muscle of the abdomen and, using your knife between those two fingers, slit open the skin all the way down to the breast bone. By making sure that your fingers lead the way in pulling the skin away from the flesh you should prevent the abdominal wall being punctured at this stage. Continue slitting the skin all the way up over the sternum, along the throat and up to the chin.

Excise the skin away from the incision on both sides of the cut then carefully pierce the abdomen taking care not to rupture any internal organs. At this point there is likely to be an expulsion of gases from the abdominal cavity. Continue the cut along the ventral line of the body all the way up to and including the throat. When you have exposed the trachea and the oesophagus tie off the latter and free it of connective tissue.

The breast bone or sternum should then be cut by using a bone saw along its length, thereby exposing the pleural cavity from

This diagram shows the meat cuts available on wild boar

Chapter 5   HUNTING WILD BOAR IN BRITAIN: THE EVENT

Boars are too hairy for their skin to be cooked – the skin is thus removed before cooking

which the heart, lungs and trachea can be removed. Removal of the oesophagus, stomach and viscera is now made relatively easy.

Once the internal organs have been removed they should be inspected for signs of abnormality or disease. If anything is suspected as not being quite right it should be bagged and sent to your local government animal health department.

If the carcase looks in generally poor condition it might be discarded and considered unfit for human consumption. Lymph glands should be small and pink as opposed to swollen and red. The liver should be smooth without lumps or discolouration. The lungs should be uniformly pink with no cysts or scars. The heart and kidneys should be without any abnormalities.

Unlike pork, the skin from a wild boar is too thick and hairy to be cooked and allowed to go crispy and so the animal is skinned before cooking rather than simply being de-bristled.

RIFLECRAFT AND STALKING TIPS
Keep your rifle clean

There must be more ways to clean a firearm than there are ways to bake a cake, and just like baking a cake there is no single correct method. However there are one or two points that need special attention because like all mechanical things they demand regular and proper maintenance. All firearms require good cleaning and lubrication after use to keep their operational performance at a peak. A firearm can get a basic clean in five quick steps.

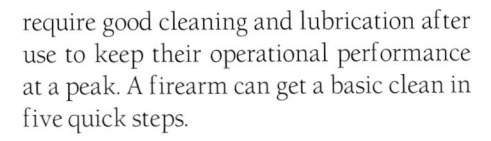

1. Unload and remove bolt

Before cleaning any gun, open the action to make sure it's unloaded. Remove the magazine and the bolt. Brush the bolt with solvent, clean, dry off, and lightly lube the bolt and extractor. Make sure you brush the magazine out as well.

2. Clean the bore

Set the cleaned bolt aside and then, always working from the breech end, run a cleaning rod with attached bronze brush soaked in gun solvent down the barrel and out the muzzle. Repeat this same action if the barrel is particularly dirty. Leave it for 10-15 minutes allowing the solvent to dissolve and soften any lead or copper residue from the bullet material, as well as powder fowling.

3. Scrub bore

After the solvent has been left soaking for a while, run the solvent soaked bronze brush down the barrel again several times to loosen any fowling in the barrel. Purists would say to unscrew the brush at the muzzle after each stroke of the cleaning rod rather than pulling it back up and out from the breach. So I must not be a purist as I do not go to such lengths.

Next I run a cloth patch through the bore to push any excess carbon out the muzzle, but this time I do not pull the patch back out. Take it off the rod, put on a clean one, and then pull the rod back out the breach end. Repeat this part of the process if you are not satisfied that it is clean

4. Clean bore with patches

Just run several solvent soaked patches down the barrel and out through the muzzle. Replace each time with a clean patch, and repeat until the patch comes out quite clean. They may never come out completely white, but if they come out black, with shades of blue and green, then keep cleaning.

Solvent can turn a lot of barrel fouling a bluish green colour. If this continues, you may need to go back to step three: soak the barrel again, leave it for 20 minutes, and then brush again.

5. Apply oil

Most shooters understand that guns do not perform well swimming in oil. After all the cleaning and scrubbing, the barrel just needs a light coat of rust preventing oil, as does the bolt. Use a clean, soft cotton cloth with oil to wipe down all the metal surfaces of the gun.

Unlike the solvent it will do no harm if you get some oil on the stock. You might also want to dust off the areas around the scope mounts, trigger and up into the action from the magazine well with a small brush.

Fight against rust

The bluing on your rifle's barrel alone will not protect it from rust, other than the fact that it is able to retain any oil that you might have applied to it. The problem is that oil will only protect the metal for a short time.

One solution that you might want to consider is the application of some floor wax, especially in areas where the metal comes into contact with the stock. Remember too, that body fluids, such as sweat from your hands, will promote rusting, which is why serious collectors always handle their weapons with cotton gloves. Dirty guns will rust more than clean ones because moisture will be attracted to dirt.

Once pitting starts as a result of rusting a gunsmith will need to be employed to deal with the problem. The moral here is, if you have been hunting in the rain make sure that you wipe your rifle down before dealing with your own creature comforts.

Accuracy

There are three things that that are of paramount importance in the manufacture of a supremely accurate rifle: these are rigidity, concentricity and minimal stress. Bench rest shooters discovered many years ago that the recoil on a bolt action rifle makes the weapon flex and create unwanted forces on the receiver. This movement within the load bearing parts of the rifle did its part in preventing really tight groups. The marksmen reacted to this by welding strengthening plates on the actions to give the weapon added strength. Modern rifles are made with this in mind and have receivers that are cylindrical in cross section and have minimal amounts of steel removed for magazine access and bolt lug guides.

Equally the barrel undergoes tremendous vibration in the form of a sine wave each time a bullet travels along its length. The less this happens the more accurate the gun will be. A short, heavy barrel will move in this way far less than long, thin one.

Concentricity pretty well speaks for itself. If components are not put together with precision and perfectly in line with one an other the rifle will clearly not perform well. In other words, barrels must screw into receivers in absolute alignment, just as the bullet must be accurately centred in the bore when the cartridge is seated in the chamber. Anything less and the firearm will lose accuracy.

Finally stress in a rifle is caused by inconsistent and excessive vibration, as well as uneven pressures on different parts of the gun during the firing process. It can be eliminated by having all parts fitting together correctly and to within the designed tolerances.

Triggers

If you have to squeeze too hard to release the trigger you will not be able to shoot accurately. The same will be true if there is too much creep or travel in trigger movement.

Barrels

A cheaply made barrel may have inconsistencies in rifling grooves and lands, this will affect tight grouping.

Lock time

This is the delay between the sear releasing the firing pin and the primer igniting. A long lock time will lead to the user flinching, which will have disastrous effect on aim.

Bedding

Modern floating barrels are fixed at one end to the chamber and the rest of the tube is designed to simply wave around at will when the gun is fired. The thinking is that if nothing interferes with this free movement then it will be the same every time and, as we have already learned, consistency is good. A poorly fitted stock that touches the barrel at any point along its length will be hopelessly inaccurate.

Trigger control

As already mentioned, the pressure needed to release the trigger is most important when attempting consistently accurate shots. It should have a pull pressure of no less than three pounds and no more than four. It should have minimal travel and should feel smooth without creep or unevenness.

When you are happy that your trigger is as it should be you then have to learn how to use it to the best of your ability. There are two schools of thought about how you should squeeze your well-tuned trigger.

The military tend to favour the method by which when you have acquired your target, you take a deep breath then exhale half of that volume and hold the rest of your breath until you have fired the shot. This tends to put you on the clock because you will have less than 10 seconds before your eyes start to blur and you will begin to sense the muzzle waving uncontrollably. With this method you have to discipline yourself to get the shot off quickly as you would with a snap shot. If you delay you will miss.

The other method is to acquire the target, but this time control your breathing and allow the rifle to gently rise up and down as you inhale and exhale. This movement should be almost imperceptibly small. As the crosshairs move up and down over the target in rhythm with your breathing you gentle squeeze the trigger as they pass over the point of aim on your exhalation. Over time you train yourself to squeeze the trigger at the same point every time during your outward breath. These methods can be practised by dry firing your rifle at home.

Recoil

It is important to use a rifle that you feel comfortable with and one that does not make you tense up just at the thought of the punch you're going to get when you fire it. Obviously some folk are tougher than others where this is concerned, but it is also true to say that some rifles are simply more vicious than others in the same calibre. I recall many years ago I owned two weapons chambered for .458 Winchester, one of which was a Brno and the other a Ruger No.1 Jungle Carbine, and as you might expect both carried quite a punch. The Brno is one that I still own today and take to Africa every time I go; the Ruger on the other hand, while being a fine rifle, in that calibre was, as far as I am concerned, just down right nasty. There are two kinds of recoil: one is real and can be measured in foot pounds, the other is perceived and is conditional upon two things. One is what you are shooting at; I will guarantee that when shooting at a paper target the recoil will be far greater than when shooting at an animal. The other thing is the design and make-up of the rifle. Neither of these two perceived recoils can be measured, but they are able to affect the way we shoot.

Recoil can be lowered using the following two accessories. A recoil pad can replace the standard butt plate on your rifle. It's softer, which will help absorb some of the energy created by the recoil. You could also use a muzzle brake. The great disadvantage in using a muzzle brake is the increase in noise that is produced as well as the fact that it really needs to be fitted by a gunsmith. They are sometimes accused of causing more fouling, which will affect accuracy as well. The good news however – they really do lower the recoil.

Stalking sticks

If you do choose to stalk your wild boar as opposed to waiting in ambush for it then you will be well advised to take along a shooting stick. Quite often when stalking wild boar in woodland they will surprise you by jumping up in front of you and running away, which means that the only hope of shooting it will be at quite close range with a reflex-driven snap shot. If, however, you spot the animal without it knowing that you are there, then all

Chapter 5   HUNTING WILD BOAR IN BRITAIN: THE EVENT

Image credit: Heather Pilbeam

Shooting off sticks will secure your rifle in the vertical plane

movements made by you, the stalker, must be kept to a minimum, and of course there is never anything close at hand on which to rest on when you really need it. It's at just such a time when a shooting stick becomes invaluable. Commercially they come in all shapes and sizes, from fold away tripods to simple sticks with a piece of antler on top.

The stick is ideal to walk with, but remember when using it rest your rifle on it is only stable in a vertical plane, it will still tend to sway from side to side unless you can really push it well into the ground.

Protect your hearing

Every shot that you ever fire will damage your hearing; sometimes, as in my case, permanently. When I started shooting it was not fashionable to do something as sensible as protect one's hearing and I have paid the price.

The first thing that can be done is to have your rifle threaded to take a moderator. There are two types of moderator, ones that fit over the barrel and those that fit on the end of the muzzle. Some of them are able to be dismantled for cleaning, although I am not altogether sure that is such a good idea, unless of course it is to clean off rust, and others that do not come apart. Choosing the right moderator is ultimately is down to personal choice and will probably end up being a compromise between length, weight, efficacy and price. One thing to remember, especially if you also use a bipod, is you are beginning to add an awful lot of extra weight to your set-up, especially if you already have a scope attached. This will be a big disadvantage if you will be carrying your weapon for any length of time, and needless to say will compromise manoeuvrability.

There are several well-known makes of moderator, but my personal preference is the A-Tech CMM4. For a start it is more compact than one or two others that are on the market today, and I have never had an A-Tech rust on me like one particular brand that I could but will not name. The A-Tec weighs just 220 grams as opposed to well over 500 grams for a moderator such as the T.8, for example.

The other precaution is of course to wear a good set of ear defenders. Some years ago I attended a clinic at my local hospital in the hope that something could be done about my failing hearing. The consultant explained to me that the damage caused by shooting both in the military and as a civilian instructor and range conducting officer was making certain frequencies of sound totally inaudible to me. In practical terms, I had no functioning nerves left to deal with those frequencies that allowed me to hear the sound of consonants in speech – and there was nothing that could be done about it. Even a hearing aid would only work for the undamaged neurones, but the non-functioning ones were incapable of picking up sound no matter how much it was amplified. The consultants advice was that I should go out and buy myself the Rolls Royce of ear defenders. Though it wouldn't make a jot of difference to what I could hear, it would at least stop matters getting any worse. That is the advice that I would pass on to readers of this book, but ideally do it before any harm has been done.

Smoking

This is frowned upon by many people for many different reasons, but I don't see it as being a problem when hunting deer or wild boar. The simple reason why people oppose it is if the wild boar can smell your smoke they will be able to smell you. The answer is to always be right winded.

American hunters in particular are very conscious about giving their position away due to the animal picking up their scent, and many will go to great trouble to ensure that they only wear Scent-Lok clothing and will wash in Scent-Lok soap. I must admit that I am slightly sceptical about the efficacy of such practices, but if it really does work then I can see that smoking wouldn't be compatible with the wearing of such clothes. The reason I say that is because it is always possible that a change in wind direction could give you away whether you are smoking or not, but if you and your clothes are scent free then the only give away when the wind changes direction is your cigarette smoke.

My biggest concern with smoking would be that a carelessly thrown cigarette butt could easily start a fire in dry weather, but I know of many very successful deer hunters who would not dream of going stalking without their cigs.

Shooting positions

If only all shots could be taken from a high seat, with a nice solid rest for the rifle, set at just the right height to suit your stature, and all the time in the world to make it. Sadly not all hunting is like that, and all too often good old compromise

Chapter 5   HUNTING WILD BOAR IN BRITAIN: THE EVENT

The author demonstrates a sitting shot

must be relied upon to take the shot. For those opportunistic shots that need to be taken when there is no support other than the ground or your own body, it pays to practice two or three shooting positions that you can use on any occasion with a degree of confidence.

Standing freehand or snap shot
Nobody really likes taking this kind of shot, but remarkably, with a bit of practise, it can be highly effective. The first principle of the snap shot has got to be: shoot fast. Make sure that your trigger arm is more or less parallel to the ground and that the rifle butt is pushed well into the shoulder. Your other arm, the one that is supporting the forend, should be directly under the rifle for maximum stability. This is not a position that can be

held for very long, and so the longer that you procrastinate over the shot the more fatigued you will feel. Remember the first principle: shoot fast.

Sitting
This can be a good, steady position to use, but it can sometimes take too long to get comfortable, and of course you will lose elevation. The important point when using the sitting position is to rest your elbow on the flesh of your leg just behind the knee. Do not allow your elbow rest on the knee itself. Bone against bone will cause wobble. If you are flexible enough you may find it better to raise your knees with both feet flat on the ground about a foot apart; then, instead of resting the forend of your rifle in your hand, cradle it in the crook of your arm while resting that arm on your raised knees. By gripping your legs with the hand of your cradle arm, you will ensure a rock steady support for your rifle. I know one or two military snipers who used this position to good effect, but I must admit they were supple and not carrying any extra weight around the waist.

Kneeling
Unlike the sitting position, this is one to get into very fast. You are able to retain a good deal of elevation and will be very steady if done correctly. For a right-handed rifleman your right buttock should rest on your right raised heel, and the triceps of your left arm should rest on your left raised knee. As with the sitting position, the bone of your elbow should not be in contact with the bone of your knee cap. A sling on the rifle may be of help in this position.

Prone
This must be one of the steadiest positions of all, unfortunately, it is all too often impossible to use because of its many drawbacks. First off, you put yourself so close to the ground that that there is nearly always something between the muzzle and the target. If you are using a firearm with any recoil to speak of you will feel every foot pound of the punch it produces because the position does not allow your body to flex in order to absorb the reaction. Older shooters may find it difficult to lift their head back sufficiently, especially if the shot being taken is slightly uphill; even younger, more flexible shooters must be sure to have enough eye relief to prevent the scope giving them a bloody eye.

To get the best advantage of this position the rifle should be raised with something other than a wobbly, often overstretched left arm (for a right-handed shooter). A Harris bipod fits the bill perfectly, but a rock or, better still, a back pack will give the rifle the support it will need. Getting comfortable in this position is important, as is being able to get comfortable before your wild boar has lost interest and wandered off. Instead of lying flat on the ground with both legs splayed out it might be better to bring your right leg out and up towards your chest. This will have the effect of raising your body slightly and therefore lessening the effect of heartbeat and breathing on your steady aim.

THE USE OF DOGS

Since the 1980s when wild boar began to re-establish themselves in the UK, the practice of hunting them with hounds, in the same way that, for example, foxes are hunted, has never been an issue. Over the years I have heard of one or two groups trying to organise such an event, but I have never heard that there had been a successful outcome. This may have been partly due to the difficulty in obtaining permission to carry out this type of hunting on the

Chapter 5: HUNTING WILD BOAR IN BRITAIN: THE EVENT

Dogs are used in boar hunting more frequently on the continent

few areas in the country where wild boar abound, and partly because taken over the country as a whole there are probably just not enough wild boar out there for it to catch on.

Historically, hunting with dogs has been widely practised across rural Britain, which has involved the pursuit and usually killing of animals with one or more dogs, frequently followed by riders on horseback. The usual quarry for this type of hunting has traditionally been foxes, deer, hares and mink, but never, as a rule, wild boar.

In recent years this type of hunting has been regarded a recreational pastime, a pest control measure, or a cruel and inhumane blood sport. Although all forms of hunting are controversial, fox hunting was the most widespread form of hunting with dogs, and as such, has been the focus of public and political attention.

Hunting with dogs has been a rural activity for centuries. The development of modern fox hunting probably came about after the Restoration in 1660, and was modelled on the royal sport of stag hunting. When stag hunting declined in the 18th century, fox hunting took over in popularity. Some landowners traditionally welcomed hunts on their land as a pest control measure, but others believe that the environmental damage caused by the hunt outweighed any pest control benefits.

In recent years, hunting with dogs has been one of the most contentious issues in modern politics and has been hotly debated in parliament for decades. Tony Blair's New Labour government took up the fight in the late 1990s, presumably in an effort to consolidate the 'townie' vote that he so craved. New Labour's 1997 manifesto promised MPs a free vote on a ban on hunting with hounds, and a large number of Labour MPs were very keen to use the party's majority to ban hunting. Not having the success they had hoped for at that time, MPs then sought to ban hunting through a number of private members' bills, which failed for lack of parliamentary time.

In 1999, with no free vote on a ban having appeared, the government appointed the Burns Inquiry to investigate the practical aspects of the different types of hunting with dogs. The remit of the Burns Inquiry was to study the implications of a ban and how any ban might be implemented. The inquiry was not asked to judge whether hunting was cruel.

The report was published in 2000, and was immediately seized on by both sides with each claiming that it validated their argument. On animal welfare, the Burns report did conclude that hunting "seriously compromises the welfare of the fox," but suggested that other methods such as using shotguns during the day or snaring could be considered equally cruel.

The focus in parliament, as well as in the public eye, was on fox hunting and still no mention of wild boar was made. In response to the Burns report the government pursued a number of bills that would give parliament a free vote on a number of options: an outright ban, hunting with regulations, and maintaining the status quo. In each case the bill failed due to irreconcilable differences and the impossibility of getting a bill that satisfied both houses.

The arguments continued going backwards and forwards between the House of Commons and the House of Lords until a new hunting bill was introduced in December 2002 that would ban stag hunting and hare coursing and introduce a system of licensing for fox hunting.

Hunts would be eligible to register if they could show that hunting was undertaken for purposes specific to pest control (the utility test), and that it would cause less suffering than any alternative method of pest control (the cruelty test).

Chapter 5 — HUNTING WILD BOAR IN BRITAIN: THE EVENT

Dachshunds are versatile hunting dogs with a good nose and a solid hunting instinct

This bill, however, met opposition in the Commons and the Lords. The Commons amended the bill to push for an outright ban, but this was then amended to a licensing system by the Lords. It was then re-amended to a ban by the Commons, before being finally rejected by the Lords. Eventually, the bill ran out of time.

Hunting with dogs was banned in Scotland by a 2002 Act of the Scottish Parliament, which was two years in the completion.

A bill was finally forced through parliament on 18 November 2004, stipulating a full ban on fox hunting, deer hunting with hounds and hare coursing. That's a part of history that I am sure many readers will remember – so where do we stand with hunting wild boar with dogs.

According to DEFRA, exemptions in the Hunting Act allow some activities to take place in limited circumstances, these are: flushing out, use of dogs below ground, to protect birds being kept or preserved for shooting, hunting rats and rabbits, retrieval of hares which have been shot, the recapture of wild animals, and final research.

So what about wild boar? I was once involved in an incident where, allegedly, some hunting with hounds had taken place. During the discussions that followed I was questioned by wildlife police officers and representatives from DEFRA in order to discover if what I had been involved in was in fact an illegal activity. I am happy to say that I was able to prove that what I had been doing was perfectly legal and in fact the incident that I had been accused of was as a result of erroneous reporting by a national newspaper. However during the meeting in which I was interviewed, I was told by a ministry veterinary surgeon that if I had been hunting wild boar with dogs, "the incident would have to be investigated further," although they were "unsure whether in fact any crime would have been committed." The act, it would seem, was not really clear, even to the 'experts'.

The Act states that flushing wild boar with dogs is acceptable, but what makes it a disaster waiting to happen is the restriction of the number of hounds allowed to be used.

A pack of foxhounds would certainly flush the boar into the open but the sense of using these dogs with firearms has got to be questioned. Moreover, the point is that a pack of any dogs cannot be used; the number is restricted to two.

A wild boar is likely to stand its ground with just one or two dogs in pursuit, but even if they are successful in flushing their quarry into the open it is likely that the dogs will be snapping at close quarters around the boar's heels. This does not make for safe shooting, and the dogs, sooner or later, will be killed either by a stray bullet or by the tusks of the boar.

In Europe some hunters would favour the use of short-legged dogs such as terriers or tekkels, which undoubtedly will make the chase slower and tend to make the distance covered shorter. Popular among the small breeds would be the fox terrier, which is commonly used in France, while the German hunting terrier is a favourite in the dog's eponymous country. Both of these terriers hunt with passion and determination, and despite their small size they are versatile, fearless hunters.

The tekkel or dachshund is one of the most versatile hunting dogs there is, with a good nose and plenty of instinct for the chase.

The use of dogs during wild boar hunts is a contentious issue

WILD BOAR – A BRITISH PERSPECTIVE

Chapter 5: HUNTING WILD BOAR IN BRITAIN: THE EVENT

The Definition of Hunting with Dogs

The issue of accurately defining 'hunting with dogs' has been raised following correspondence between a West Country landowner and DEFRA, and the acquittal of a hunt master accused of breaking the Scottish anti-hunting legislation.

The following paper, written by Jim Barrington, who at the time chaired the Middle Way group, explains some of the difficulties in distinguishing between actions that are legal and illegal:

"Hunting with dogs has never been properly defined. The original Bill to ban hunting in 1997 attempted a series of definitions, such as 'to pursue, harry, catch etc.', but these definitions were removed due to a failure to come to an agreed form of words that properly described the offence. Since then, a simplified version has been used in Bills and relies upon the courts to show intention to hunt.

The offence stated in Clause 1 of the Hunting Act is: "A person commits an offence if he hunts a wild mammal with a dog, unless his hunting is exempt". However, the Act does not define 'hunting with dogs' and, since it is the dog that hunts, it is unclear exactly what the human has to do in order to commit an offence. Other actions, such as 'flushing' out of 'cover', are also not defined. To add to the confusion, DEFRA added another phrase - 'chasing away' of wild mammals with dogs- though again such a definition is not included by the Hunting Act.

The League Against Cruel Sports holds the view that merely chasing a wild mammal with dogs accurately defines hunting, but can the offence be that simple, given that there is a range of actions that involve the use of dogs, some pursuing wild mammals?

Illegal Hunting

Even if it can be shown that it was the intention of the person or persons in control of the dogs to deliberately hunt a wild mammal (other than those exempt species), there will be further problems. Combating rural crime is already a very difficult problem and without proper definitions of the offence, policing a ban will be almost impossible.

Exactly who is committing the offence? The Huntsman? The Master? Anyone in control of the dogs? Anyone following the hunt (bearing in mind that any follower can point to where an animal has run and thereby could be argued to be taking part in the hunt)?

- At what point in the hunt is the offence committed?
- Are the Police prepared to seize 40 or 50 dogs and any number of horses used in a hunt, as they are permitted to do in Clause 8 of the Act?
- Will a wild mammal have to be produced to show that an offence has been committed?
- Will this be an offence?

Exempt Hunting

Some hunts have stated that they will continue operating in very much the same way as before the ban was introduced but, instead, will be hunting one or both of the exempt species, ie. rats and rabbits included in Schedule I of the Hunting Act. To the observer, however, the whole operation may look exactly the same as a traditional hunt.

Drag Hunting

Drag hunts look and operate in very much the same way as traditional quarry hunts, with the exception that the hounds are following a scent trail laid by a human. Once again, the observer would find the difference between a drag hunt and a quarry hunt very difficult.

Exercising Hounds

Certain hunts will not wish to dispose of their hounds and have stated that they will continue to keep their packs to preserve the bloodlines. These animals will continue to be exercised and the Hunting Act does not prevent those in control of the hounds from riding or wearing red coats. Once again, to the observer, this will be extremely difficult to distinguish from other forms of organised hunting, unless it can be shown that a wild mammal is being intentionally hunted.

Chasing Away

Initially, DEFRA has stated that a landowner who uses his four dogs to frighten foxes and deer off his land would be committing an offence under the Hunting Act. These animals attack his livestock and damage his woodland and he has been undertaking this effective, but non-lethal, form of pest control for the past six years. However, the Act makes it an offence for anyone to hunt a wild mammal with a dog unless it is 'exempt hunting' (which permits the flushing to guns of an animal by 2 dogs only). This obliged the landowner to use only two of his four dogs at any one time. It also put him in the ridiculous position of being legally obliged to purchase a high-powered rifle and to shoot any animal 'flushed' by his dogs.

Faced with the landowner's complaint about this ridiculous situation, a DEFRA lawyer then advised that he was merely 'chasing away unwanted animals' from his land and that this was not, in fact, hunting as described in the Hunting Act 2004. Therefore, this was not an offence.

Following numerous media reports on this apparently enormous loophole in the Act, DEFRA officials have changed their minds yet again. Despite the landowner clearly stating in numerous e-mails and telephone conversations that his four dogs 'chase' away the foxes and deer, DEFRA have written to him saying that they were under the impression that there was no chase involve and that dogs were only barking at the wild mammals. The landowner is naturally exasperated at this latest view and disputes that DEFRA did not know that his dogs were involved in a chase.

By any normal use of the word 'chase', one would understand this to mean a pursuit of some kind (dictionary definitions: pursue, run after, hunt, hound, follow, trail, track, look for, search for, go after, go in pursuit of).

Searching

Following the introduction of the Protection of Wild Mammals (Scotland) Act 2002, a high-profile test case was brought against the master of the Buccleuch Fox Hounds for hunting a fox. The master was acquitted, with the judge stating that he had not broken the law and had been 'searching' for a fox with the intention to shoot it, as permitted under the Act. The case added yet another version, albeit under the Scottish legislation, to a growing list of activities involving the chasing of wild mammals with dogs in one form or another.

Unintentional Hunting

In any of the above scenarios, a wild mammal could be unintentionally hunted. The DEFRA website explains what will happen if dogs taking part in a drag hunt kill a fox. DEFRA states that this will not be an offence 'because people will only be hunting when they, themselves, intend to pursue the quarry animal'. In other words, if there is no intention to hunt then there is no crime. However, this can equally apply to any of the other forms of chasing wild mammals mentioned above."

The above pretty well sums things up, although as wild boar have never even been mentioned in the Act, other than the indirect reference by way of the fact that they are mammals, should we regard them more as rats and rabbits, in which case they are exempt from the act, or should we treat them as foxes or deer, so they are fully protected by the act?

Chapter 5 — HUNTING WILD BOAR IN BRITAIN: THE EVENT

Labradors are strong all-rounders, combining brains and brawn

The breed has its origins in Germany and is bred in three sizes. Their hunting ability is extensive and they show a great deal of enthusiasm for the hunt.

Other hunters in mainland Europe would prefer to use more long legged, powerful dogs that will cover large distances such as hounds like the Grand Griffon Vendéen or the St Hubert hound. Pointers are frequently used to course the boar rather than pursuing them over long exhausting distances.

My use of dogs in the pursuit of wild boar is rather more limited, as might be expected in the UK. In fact the dog that I have used most extensively for both deer and wild boar has been the labrador. I still have a bitch that featured in one of the stories of wild boar hunts in this book and she must be one of the best dogs that I have ever seen working with pigs. She is old now and living a life of Riley in retirement, but in her day she was tireless in carrying out her work, which was quite often to blood scent wounded animals and on occasions to flush them.

She grew up with wild boar and deer and understood them intimately. I have seen her get tossed 10 feet in the air by a sow, return to Earth and continued almost as though nothing had happened.

On another memorable occasion she was attacked and trampled by a cow elk, which resulted in her back leg being broken in multiple places. Metal scaffolding kept the bone fragments locked in place for six weeks while she healed, but even during her recovery she longed to be back out on the hill and had to be physically restrained from breaking her regime of kennel rest.

In the course of her duty I have watched her on more than one occasion bring down an injured roe buck that had gone to ground after being shot, as well as finding wild boar that we had given up as lost after being shot in thick cover.

This was her life, and these events were a part of her every day existence. So many times I thought I knew best and would try to make her look elsewhere or put her onto a different scent when we had trouble finding a lost beast, but finally I learned to trust her and she never let me down.

Labradors are certainly not specialist trackers, such as the Bavarian mountain hounds or the Hanoverian scenthound, but they are great all-rounders with an excellent nose and enough weight behind them to get stuck in when the occasion needs a wee bit of brawn as well as brain.

WILD BOAR – A BRITISH PERSPECTIVE

TALES OF BOAR HUNTS

Barbara Sackman, a prolific trophy hunter from New York, enjoyed a boar hunt in south-west Scotland

For me all hunting trips are memorable, but it goes without saying that some have reasons for being that little bit extra special and come to mind more easily than others. Over the years I can recall many such occasions that have been outstanding or even unique, and not always because of a successful outcome.

I often think of a wild boar hunting expedition to Germany where I spent one night in a high seat that was so lavish that it came not only with a bed, but also heating and was of better quality than some hotels I have had the dubious pleasure of staying at.

On the second night of this same trip I had the misfortune of being at a different location where the high seat was just that – a seat strapped to a tree where I spent the entire night watching for my prey to venture close enough for me to take a shot in temperatures that exceeded minus 20°C. Despite having some good clothing and encasing myself in a four season sleeping bag, I could not prevent myself from shivering the whole night long.

On both occasions I failed to even see a wild boar, let alone get a shot at one, and yet in retrospect I look back with fond memories at that time and recall the good friends with whom I was reunited in the morning and with whom experiences were exchanged.

I also have some great memories of hunts where I have guided clients, and although I did not actually squeeze the trigger myself, I shared the excitement that was enjoyed by other people.

One such client was Ralph, a hunter from Alabama who had spent two weeks with me on different occasions searching for hunting trophies throughout the UK.

Here is Ralph's story along with three other memorable accounts of wild boar hunting in south-west Scotland.

WILD BOAR, ROE BUCKS, AND DOUBLE TRIGGERS

I first met Ralph Marcum at a Safari Club International fund raiser in Birmingham, Alabama, where, at the time, he was the president of that chapter. Ralph is a giant of a man both in stature and status, and at first I found him slightly intimidating, making our conversation somewhat inhibited.

Of course it should be mentioned that I had heard a lot about Ralph and his hunting companion Roger Barker many times before actually meeting them, and all of the stories were of how these two men were prolific hunters and were known for the many awards they had won for their contribution towards hunting and conservation. Needless to say both

The double triggers that foxed Ralph

Chapter 6: TALES OF WILD BOAR HUNTS

men had hunted just about everywhere in the world, for all types of game, including the big five, and with outfitters, some of whom are the best in the business. Indeed Roger owns great deal of land in Alabama where he has a breeding programme for whitetail deer.

I had been told that they were seriously interested in hunting in the UK and now they were quizzing me on the possibility of guiding them for the quarry species that they were after.

Arrangements were made and 18 months later the two men and their wives were over here in the UK with a number of species on their list. It was their intention to do a European 'grand slam' of trophies from England and Scotland. We were successful in England hunting for muntjac, Chinese water deer, fallow, red, and Japanese sika, before moving north of the border to Scotland where we would be looking for red deer, roe deer and of course, wild boar.

It was late September, and I had taken Ralph out for three consecutive days searching for a good representative roebuck without any luck. We had seen any number of does, but, as is often the case at that time of year, the mature bucks were proving to be highly elusive.

This was our sixth outing, the afternoon of the third day, and we set off hoping that this time we would be lucky. I was heading for a high seat in a woodland on the edge of the Galloway hills in Kirkcudbrightshire. As we made our way to the location that backed on to an old established wood, things suddenly began to happen. We were making our way through an immature Sitka spruce plantation keeping tightly to the edge of a wide firebreak that led us to a stretch of deer fence that ran perpendicular to our advance. As we got close to the fence and the corner of this block of trees I edged cautiously forward not wanting to scare off anything that might be around the corner in either direction. Looking to the right along a path running next to the fence and about 75 metres away, stood a magnificent buck totally oblivious of our approach. That was about to change.

Now it has to be said that the terrain that we were covering was quite hard going, with lots of thick grassy tussocks and uneven ground. As I have already said, Ralph is a big man and he was never going to move fast. However I urged him to come forward as quickly and quietly as possible while at the same time handing him my .243 Mannlicher-Schoenauer rifle complete with a double set trigger.

Looking back I should have realised that from the moment I spotted this fine buck the whole episode was doomed to failure. Had we been comfortably established in our high shooting box, things could have worked out well, but as it turned out I can sometimes still hear that buck laughing at us.

In his eagerness, big Ralph almost felled two medium-sized trees as he bounced from one to the other in an effort to get to a firing position. As he raised the rifle I could see that he was fumbling uncomfortably with the two triggers. The trigger configuration is a European innovation and not really intended for our American cousins who, not wanting to multitask, prefer to concentrate on just the one lever.

As I watched him getting more stressed I realised that unless he had worked incredibly fast without my noticing, I was sure that he had not chambered a round. All of this happened in less than a heartbeat, but as I watched on, it was as though time had slowed down. I looked at the buck who seemed to be quite relaxed and watching us uncertainly, or more likely disbelieving what he was seeing. The buck turned to face the fence, his nose almost touching the wire. I knew we were fast running out of time. The buck glanced back at us for one last look, probably to reassure himself that he was not imagining these two 'good old boys' acting as though they had just spent an afternoon consuming copious quantities of moonshine. "He's going to jump," was all I could think to say. "Just put a round in the chamber and shoot it," I said in a stifled whisper. It was too late. The buck leapt the high fence and once on the other side looked back at us barked once and then slowly melted into the old wood.

Ralph and I looked at each other his brow deeply furrowed in a troubled frown. I felt reasonably confident that he was considering inserting my Mannlicher into a place where, despite what I may believe to the contrary, I am assured the sun does not shine. As I watched Ralph, waiting for him to explode, I saw his whole demeanour change. His face began to glow and his eyes widened. Ralph slowly and purposefully raised the rifle, and this time I clearly saw him chamber a round.

At first I thought perhaps he had second thoughts about using my rifle as a suppository and was simply going to shoot me instead. Then I realised that he was not looking at me, but just over my left shoulder instead. I turned, half expecting to see another buck coming out of the cover of the young sitka spruce plantation. Imagine my surprise when, as I turned slowly around, not 50 metres away a huge wild boar was walking out of the trees and into the open totally oblivious of our presence. These creatures do not have good eyesight, but this big boy must surely have been deaf as well.

As I took in exactly what I was looking at, I realised that this was not the run of the mill wild boar that we frequently see in this area. This was an animal that was probably going to weigh far in excess of 350lb, and even with a cursory glance I could see his enormous tusks.

"OK, Ralph. Take your time, remember pull the back trigger first, then, when you are good and ready, you only have to touch the front one to fire the weapon," I whispered, concerned that we were undergunned for a pig this size.

"Wait until he turns and his near front leg is moved forwards and that's the place to nail him," I said. I could see Ralph struggling to get comfortable, so I assertively dug a full length bi-pod into the ground in front of him. Now he was set. A look of calmness came over his face, followed by his whole body becoming one with his rifle. For some reason when he fired it came as something of a surprise

Ralph may have missed his chance to grab a roebuck, but lady luck smiled on the hunter just minutes later

Chapter 6   TALES OF WILD BOAR HUNTS

to me; the sound and shock waves physically shaking me. The big boar just ran back into cover and at first I thought he must have missed. We both cautiously moved forward, when suddenly the boar broke out of the trees not 15 metres away and was heading in our direction at some speed. I have shot many wild boar, but have never had a reaction quite like this one. I felt particularly vulnerable not being armed myself, but my grip tightened on the shooting stick in preparation for some close quarter combat. "Put another one into him," I said, as if Ralph needed telling. He was way ahead of me and by the time the boar was five metres closer, Ralph had shot him again in the chest, which sent him reeling off to his left and back into the wood. We stood there in silence. Ralph chambered an insurance round as we stood there listening for the giveaway sound of breaking branches or other indications of the boars whereabouts.

After 10 minutes I followed the blood trail into thick sitka trees and soon ended up on my hands and knees at the mercy of the vicious pine needles. Beneath the low branches my visibility was greatly improved, and within minutes I had located the dead animal laid up against the trunk of one of the larger trees. I reached in to the low cover in an effort to grab a leg and pull the boar into the open. As I did, the animal kicked me, which had the effect of making me leap back once again in fear of my life. The involuntary movement was just post mortem nerve impulses signalling the death of this huge beast.

I called Lyndon the estate keeper on the radio to help get the boar out of the wood. After several attempts I realised I was not going to manage to do this alone and for good reason. When we got the carcase back to the skinning shed it weighed in at 420lbs.

The tusks were measured at 10 $^{15}/_{16}$ inches for the left, 10 $^{8}/_{16}$ inches for the right, and circumferences of 2 $^{15}/_{16}$ and 2 $^{6}/_{16}$ respectively, giving a total SCI score of 26 $^{2}/_{16}$. Ralph had just shot a new European record.

Both of his shots were good ones and I am certain that the first round would have stopped any normal pig, but this really was a big boy and the .243 is not really an ideal round for that particular job. And Ralph? Well, he got his roe buck the following day and is now a convert to the double set trigger – I think.

A WILD BOAR MANAGEMENT HUNT

My gamekeeper Lyndon and I were thankful that the weather seemed to be holding up as we waited for our guests to arrive. Extracting a 400-500lb wild boar from thick cover can be challenging at the best of times, but in wet conditions when the ground becomes boggy, the task can be hellish. The threat of a heavy downpour seemed to be lessening, but in SW Scotland the weather can change almost without warning, and we are no strangers to a wee bit of precipitation in this part of the country. The conditions were now overcast, but the cloud cover was high and the day was bright; an ideal day for boar shooting.

The day's event was planned some weeks earlier when Mike McCrave, a sporting agent who, like myself, promotes hunting opportunities to the American market, phoned me to enquire about the availability of a trophy quality keiler for an American client with whom he was touring the UK.

There would be no time, or a high enough success expectation to hunt for a wild, trophy quality animal, so we would

Ralph and his 420lb boar, more than making up for the missed roebuck

Chapter 6 TALES OF WILD BOAR HUNTS

need to look in our wild boar park. This is a large densely wooded area where its inhabitants live in as close to wild conditions as possible until they are, from time to time, culled for market. This is usually when their numbers reach a level too high for the ground to sustain or other altruistic reasons.

Mike was in luck. In recent weeks we had been having a problem with a big old boar within the park who had been behaving aggressively towards other members of the herd. Several times we had witnessed a battle for dominance between this old boy and a younger rival. Power struggles such as this are not uncommon, and they are normally settled with the victor showing dominance over the less robust combatant and peace is once again restored to the group. However this time harmony was a long time coming, and it was becoming clear that the older master boar was now having his authority constantly challenged by the younger, stronger member of the pack. In the wild a defeated boar would move well away from all the others, coming into contact with them again only if they are all attracted to a common temptation such as a source of food or a female in oestrus. In park conditions this situation has to be artificially managed and, as the big male was not only sustaining injuries himself, but was also inflicting wounds on some of the smaller females and youngsters, it was fast becoming time for him to go.

Larry didn't have to wait long to spot his quarry

When Mike finally arrived he introduced Lyndon and I to his client Larry Higgins from Michigan, who as it turned out was a prolific hunter and collector of trophies and who was well known for his hunting exploits in some of the most remote places on Earth. He has hunted most of the trophy sheep species in the world, including argali, Marco Polo and all of the American big horns, leaving only the ovis found in politically inaccessible countries that have escaped appearing in his crosshairs. I, of course, was suitably miffed when he failed to appreciate the challenge of stalking one of our Soay rams!

With Larry feeling comfortable with the standard .308 Remington, modified only with an H S Precision stock, we headed out towards the park to begin our search for the troublesome porcine.

Keeping the wind in our favour took us on a slightly circuitous route through a small wood, and as I led our party forward I was keen not to push any deer ahead of us and thereby spoil our ground. Twenty minutes later we came out of the wood to where an open area either side of a re-entrant lay ahead of us. As I glassed an area 120 yards away on the other side of the small glen, I saw four or five sows digging up an area between some trees.

We probably spent the best part of half an hour watching and waiting. Suddenly our patience was rewarded, and a big mature boar came out of the wood on the far side of the hill and began pushing his weight around with the females,

Larry Higgins (right), Mike McCrave (or 'The Man in the Kilt', a well known outfitter) and Larry's fantastic boar

bullying them and taking from them any piece of ground that held the promise of a succulent root or perhaps a fat slug or tasty larvae.

Sadly though, this was not the old boy that we were after; this was the contender to his throne. We continued watching the interactions between the different members of this small group, fascinated by the small squabbles and bullying that went on in an overt display of pecking orders within the sounder.

I was so engrossed in the collection of mini dramas that were being acted out in front of me that when Lyndon tapped me on the shoulder I nearly jumped out of my skin. He pointed up to the tree line and slightly to the left. Lyndon has a particularly sharp eye and it took me a moment or two, even with the use of my binoculars to focus on what he was pointing at. It was our boar, but at first sight he was just a dark shadow beneath the low hanging branches of a sitka spruce. As we watched, he began to venture away from the tree line and down the hill towards where the others were feeding. Through my binoculars I could see a large open wound down his right flank and although it didn't seem to be causing him any great concern, I could tell it was a fresh injury and was still bleeding.

Almost imperceptibly the dynamics of the herd changed and the younger animal walked at a fast pace up the hill to meet the old master head on in a bid to subjugate him. Squealing like a pig is an apt and literal expression for what we heard as once again the two boys ran circles around each other in an effort to nail the opposition with his formidable tusks.

The battle was short lived and I quickly nodded to Larry, indicating that if he was happy with the shot I was happy that he should now terminate the old king's reign. Larry asked for confirmation that he should shoot the nearer of the two boars. He spoke in a low, calm voice as he used the branch of a tree to steady his aim.

"Yes, the one that is lower down the hill," I said as I looked again at my rangefinder. "110 yards," I whispered. When Larry took the shot, I watched with absolute clarity as the Norma 180g plastic tipped bullet hit the old warrior just behind and below the shoulder sending a shock tremor along the whole length of his body. He stood rigidly still for a moment before running up the hill and into the cover of the trees in an adrenalin-fuelled dash of death.

It took us five minutes to cross the small valley and get to the keiler that had, by now, crashed to the ground. We watched from a distance as his rear legs kicked out in several post mortem muscle spasms. The carcase was taken back to the larder and later the tusks were removed and measured. Larry was pleased with his trophy, which scored 24 SCI points and ranks in the top 20 European (estate) wild boar.

NOCTURNAL WILD BOAR

Carminnows Sporting Estate is nestled at one end of the Glenkens in SW Scotland. Local folk law claims that this location has a magical reputation for casting a spell of contentment on all who visit the area. I find this interesting because when two hunters from the south of England left after a busy weekend's sport, I swear that the look on each of their faces was just that: fulfilled contentment.

Terry Axten and his good friend Simon Harms had come north primarily to hunt the free ranging wild boar that are to be found in this area, although they had made it clear that should an opportunity for other quarry present itself they would more than up for it. This was ideal because the way we hunt the free ranging wild boar is pretty much the same as we hunt black bear in Canada, which is over baited sites. Although, unlike bear hunting, the best results with the pigs tend to be at night.

However, these boys felt that although they were prepared to stay up all night if necessary, they did not want to waste all of the daylight hours sleeping. They were here to hunt and that is what they wanted to do, so while the night time was reserved for the wild boar, during the day we were to go out in search of wild goats and possibly some cull deer on the estate. Sleep, they argued could wait until they were back at work on Monday morning.

There has been much misunderstanding and misrepresentation about what goes

Cleo, Terry and two shot boar – a good night's work

WILD BOAR – A BRITISH PERSPECTIVE

on at Carminnows, which in fact is really no different from the many deer parks and wild boar farms throughout the country. Like all of these places, whether it be a prestigious park owned by the aristocracy or a privately owned estate bordered by a high fence, herd numbers have to be kept in check and paying clients are often invited to take part in annual culls.

Unlike many of these places, Carminnows is heavily wooded and its inhabitants are as close as they can get to being totally wild without actually removing the fence. A cull on Carminnows is certainly not a matter of going in to an open field and pulling the trigger. As in the wild, on a day's hunting the odds are in favour of the quarry. Added to this there are large areas of the estate that are unfenced, which is where we stalk red and roe deer and where we encourage free ranging wild boar not only with bait sites, but with the lure of our captive sows when they come into oestrus. It should also be mentioned that these 'wild' boar are not the result of escapees or from intentional releases of our captive animals. Interestingly, the critics, conspiracy theorists and armchair plums who like to wallow with each other in their internet quagmire of fantasy are all people who have, of course, never visited the estate. Had they done so, they too, I am sure would have had the aforementioned spell of contentment cast upon them.

Both Terry and Simon were exceptional people in a time, country and sport where the essence of what we do is getting lost. Both of these lads loved their hunting and had a very serious hunting ethic, but they had not lost sight of the idea that they had also come away for a weekend's break, and they wanted to enjoy themselves. For that reason they were a pleasure to hunt with and great company into the bargain.

A lot of hunting went on that mid-September weekend, but the highlight was on the Saturday night when the two lads were taken to their respective high seats just before dusk. It was an ideal night in many respects, the temperature had not dropped too severely and the moon was in its last quarter, so there was a modicum of light. On the downside, there was the promise of rain, and at that time of year the bracken was still high, making getting a visual on an animal the height of a pig less than favourable.

Lyndon and I left the two hunters, who were about half a mile apart, to their evening's vigil with the instruction to phone should they get lucky or encounter any problems and we would be along as soon as it would take us to cover the mile and a half from the house.

After tending to the many chores that had been neglected during that day's hunting, both Lyndon and I retired to our respective quarters awaiting any communication from Terry or Simon. I had switched the TV on half an hour before and its soporific effect was just beginning to take place when suddenly the phone rattled me back to full consciousness. It was Terry. "Steve," he said, his voice full of concern. "A whole group of pigs came in and I shot one. I know that I hit it, but I can't see it from here. What should I do?"

I suggested he waited a while and not to get down from the high seat just yet. "There's not much we can do right now without spoiling the area and there is a good chance that the herd will return. Just give me a call in a while if you feel that you've had enough," I said.

It was more than an hour later when the phone rang again. Terry's voice was slightly more upbeat this time: "You were right. They did come back and this time I shot a really big one. The only problem is that I can't see this one either," he admitted with a slightly deflated edge to his voice.

"OK," I said. "Just hang on there and don't walk around too much, I'll be along with the dog."

I collected Cleo, my labrador bitch who has an enviable record of finding both lost deer and wild boar, and mounted the waiting ATV with trailer and ropes.

By the time I got to Terry's high seat, Simon had joined him and they were waiting for me to go in search of our fallen quarry. As we walked the 80 metres or so to the bait area Terry told me what had happened as the wild boar paid their two nocturnal visits to his stand. There was a degree of light banter between the two friends as Terry admitted that on the second visit he was beginning to doze off when he was awoken by a phone call from Simon, enquiring as to how he was getting along. As he was talking to Simon, Terry realised that the herd was there feeding and had it not been for Simon's wake-up call he may easily have missed this second opportunity. As soon as we neared the bait we saw the larger of the two animals laid out, partially obscured by some bracken, felled by a single clean shot through the heart.

After looking nearby for the second animal for a few minutes it seemed clear that this was not going to be quite so easy, and by now a light rain would quickly wash away any blood signs. I attached the long, flat tracking lead to Cleo's collar and in a tone with which the dog was familiar, I instructed her to find the pig.

She set off instantly and without hesitation along what looked to be a well-beaten game trail leading away from the bait area. She led me downhill and then around trees and under bushes, across streams and through the thickest bracken she could find. I was beginning to think that she was simply out to prove that she was fitter than I, or that this was some kind of retribution for something I had previously done to upset her.

I decided that Cleo was probably following a live trail rather than a blood scent, when she emerged from a tunnel of bracken and I spotted blood on her back in my torch light. I closely examined the vegetation and sure enough there was a copious amount of blood on the undersides of the bracken fronds. With renewed enthusiasm I continued following the labrador who now seemed

Simon got a boar the day after Terry shot his

to be taking me round in a great circle and crossing a path that I recalled being dragged along 20 minutes before. After another 10 minutes or so I began to lose faith in Cleo's ability once more. I truly believe that sometimes dogs can read one's mind, and just as I was thinking of calling a halt to this increasingly gruelling quest she just stopped and held her head above some low growing bracken and looked at me wagging her tail furiously. Without even seeing the fallen animal I knew that she had found it. Terry of course was delighted and Simon shot a very respectable boar the next day.

ROGUE BOAR

I usually welcome free ranging wild boar coming on to my ground, which they frequently do when food is short during the winter months. For one, clients enjoy the opportunity of being able to hunt truly wild wild boar and I personally like the idea of this newest reintroduction of all our game species coming in to our bait sites.

They are rarely seen during the daylight hours, although evidence of their nocturnal visitations can be very apparent with no room for doubt that the disturbance to the ground was caused by *Sus scrofa*.

It was of no great surprise just recently when I noticed that our bait sites were receiving some regular attention, and so I put the word out to some keen hunters on my 'short notice' list that now might be a good time for them to come along and try their luck.

The most successful method of nailing these free roaming individuals is to spend a long, cold night in a stand close to a bait site and wait for them to come in. The favourite time seems to be between two and four in the morning, and unfortunately the thought of a warm comfortable bed is too much for many hunters to endure when they have been rooted to the same spot in a blind since late afternoon the previous day.

One particular client was beginning to feel that perhaps his accommodation was far more appealing than his present arrangement when suddenly he was motivated by the unmistakeable sound of snuffling around the bait barrel.

After straining his eyes in an effort to see through the darkness without success, he decided to make use of the lamp we provided. As is often the case, even though the lamp was filtered, the effect of switching on the light was enough to make the animals run for cover. This was repeated several more times during the next two hours after which time all activity stopped, as did that night's vigil.

After a debriefing that morning I concluded that from the very brief glimpses my client got of these opportunistic feeders it was probably a sounder of females with youngsters that he had spotted.

This would in part explain why they were acting so warily and it is just such a group that we often get coming in to our bait. Lone keilers and other solitary males are less often seen.

As I said, I normally welcome these free ranging beasts about the property, but shortly after the incident just described I noticed a subtle difference in the activity of our visitors, and over the next week or so became slightly concerned at the damage that was being caused.

At first it was simply that the grass verges on the sides of the road were noticeably being ploughed up, but then on one frosty morning I saw that some deer fencing had been breached and that the highly valued grazing land that we have had also been assaulted by this unwanted four-legged farmer.

This was not the normal behaviour of our free ranging herds in the area, they are not usually so bold, and so I wondered if maybe one or two of our own captive wild boar may have escaped and be responsible.

This was a highly unlikely scenario because the herd that we keep behind a fence are in a large wooded enclosure that is not only secure, but, because the inhabitants are well fed, there is also very little incentive for them to leave. After close inspection of the fence I was totally satisfied that our animals had not got out and that it was without doubt a rogue pig hell bent on getting to either my stock's feed or to my sows that may be in oestrus. By now I believed this to be a good size solitary male.

The situation had now gone from being an opportunity for some recreational hunting to a real need to eliminate a marauding beast that was causing damage to both fencing and grazing land.

My gamekeeper and stalker Lyndon, who was of course totally up to speed with what was happening, phoned me at one point and said that I should come over to where he was. He requested that I bring along my .308 rifle and one of the dogs, as he had been inspecting some very recent ground damage and had caught sight of a good sized boar running off into the woods. Here was another move away from the normal pattern of behaviour, this time the beast was active during the day and allowed someone to get quite close before bolting away. Although we spent more than an hour searching

Tim and his Beast of Glenkens – whether it was the same boar who caused so much damage is unknown

WILD BOAR – A BRITISH PERSPECTIVE   125

Chapter 6: TALES OF WILD BOAR HUNTS

through the woods, we did not see the boar again that day.

Tim is a client who is always on the look out for something new or different, and he was due in at the end of the week. He had it in his mind to take a good soay ram, but I thought that he would be interested in helping us find this problem beast, and, if the opportunity arose, shoot it, meanwhile Lyndon and I would continue to hunt down the Beast of the Glenkens ourselves.

For the next two days we awoke to discover more damage and more fences attacked, but try as we may we could not get any closer to putting a stop to this itinerant beast's escapades.

On the third day, just as suddenly as this activity had started, it stopped, and in fact to this day, although we still get our nocturnal visitors and the occasional furrowing of good pastureland, it has not been so intense as during the week that we became the unwilling host of this rogue boar.

When Tim arrived we told him what had been happening and that he had probably just missed the drama; he was visibly disappointed to have missed out on the action.

After getting his trophy ram, Tim asked if there would be any point in going back to the stand by the bait site in the hope that this problem boar might still be in the location.

I agreed that all things are possible, but we would probably have as much chance with this particular animal by simply covering as much ground as possible in the areas that he had been before. At the same time he would have to pay attention to the large wooded area where our trophy animals are kept because I was fairly certain that it was our breeding sows that that were attracting him and made him behave in such an unusual manner.

There was no doubt that Tim was now in the mood to take a wild boar, and so it was with an optimistic heart that he set out with Lyndon in the hope of getting himself a memorable trophy. Some hours later, much to my surprise I received a phone call from Lyndon asking me to come and get them and a wild boar with the ATV and trailer.

I could not wait to get to them to hear the story, but could not help doubting that this was going to be the boar that had caused us so much trouble. When I got to them they were in the enclosed area and both were grinning from ear to ear.

Lyndon explained that they decided to walk along the side of the fenced woodland when they saw what looked like a freshly broken section of mesh and a lot of pig slots in the ground around the broken fence.

The two hunters decided to take a look and as they climbed over the fence they could hear a lot of commotion in the wood not far from where they were standing.

Creeping in for a closer look they travelled for maybe 200 yards to a clearing where several pigs were feeding. Lyndon claims that as soon as he saw one of the males he was convinced it was one that he had never seen before and told Tim that it was his if he wanted it.

Without hesitation Tim got into the prone position and chambered a round in his 7mm Rem Mag Blaser fixing his crosshairs over the heart of his first wild boar. Tim hesitated for only a second before sending a Norma 156-grain bullet to bring about this animal's demise.

Was it the villain guilty of breaking and entering and causing criminal damage? I don't know, but it proved to be an exciting afternoon's stalking and provided Tim with an excellent trophy and the game dealer with a good deal of sausage meat.

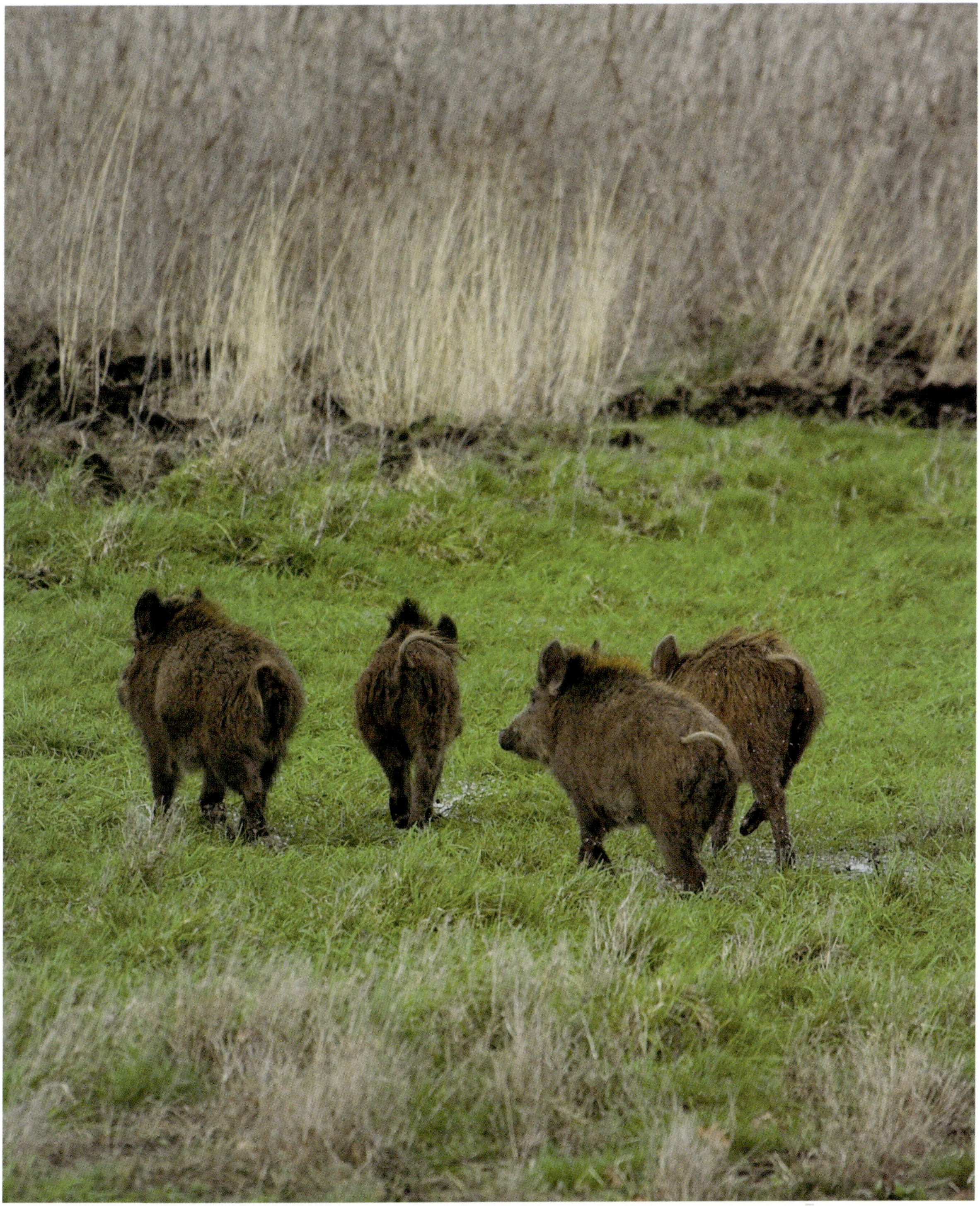

Chapter 6   TALES OF WILD BOAR HUNTS

The stories that I have recounted, while memorable, are not the only accounts of wild boar hunting that are worthy of mention. Some remain in my memory, not so much due the actual hunt, but because of the characters that took part and the circumstances or incidents that took place during my clients time with me.

One such occasion was when Safari Club International hunters Sid and Jerry Johnson came to the UK primarily with the intention of stalking roebucks, but also to take any other quarry species that I was able to get them on to. I seem to recall thinking at the time that Sid was the hunter and the little lady was just going along to keep her husband happy. It was not long before I had reason to reconsider my initial assessment.

By the second day of the hunt Sid had successfully harvested a Japanese sika that made a surprise appearance in an area that I had never before seen that particular deer species. Having finished the morning's hunting on a high note I decided to give Jerry my undivided attention that afternoon with the intention of getting her in front of a good representative buck.

I suspected this was going to be an ordeal; a contest of minds where instead of being out on the hill, she would not mind being in the cosmetic department of Debenhams and I would not mind if she told me that was where she was going.

It was not that I did not get on with her, I just felt that she was there only because her husband wanted it that way, and as such I was going to be the teacher trying to engage the enthusiasm of an uninterested and unwilling child.

I only noticed the change in her demeanour slowly, but it started soon after we had alighted from the Land Rover and I had handed her the estate rifle. Within 10 minutes of entering the woods I was aware that I was in the company of a seasoned veteran who was every bit as much of a hunter as her husband.

Having spotted a buck that we were happy with we began to stalk into a position where Jerry could take a shot. As we stood watching in silence I could feel the tension building. Jerry, who was standing slightly in front of me, slowly turned with her arm stretched out behind her in an effort to take a shooting stick from me. As she looked back at me, her expression changed to one that I can only describe as shock horror. Almost immediately I realised that she was not looking at me, but just past me over my left shoulder. I swung around and was astounded to see, standing about 40 yards away, a big keiler, head down, ears back and looking in our direction.

To say I was surprised is an understatement, but what was even more surprising was the aggression that the boar seemed to be displaying. My mind was reeling and knew that I needed to give Jerry some direction in what she should do next. However, she had already decided to forgo the buck in favour of the boar and with deadly determination stepped forward at the same time as she raised the rifle to her shoulder. Her aim was true and from a free hand position

Jerry surprised the author with her hunting prowess, and she poses with her spoils here

Jerry killed the wild boar before it was able to take a single step nearer to us.

Over dinner that night we discussed the events of the day and I was unable to answer the question as to what the boar's intentions were. It certainly looked as if it were approaching us with aggression, although I suspect it was simply curious and could not make out what these two silent invaders of its territory were all about. Jerry on the other hand adopted her alter ego once more and showed very little interest in the conversation that centred on her earlier exploits.

Another memorable character was Tony Crabb, a volley ball coach from Hawaii who flew all the way to Scotland to shoot a wild boar then packed his bags happy that he had achieved his ambition and got back on the plane for another 36 hour flight back home.

Over a two year period I offered wild boar culling to clients in order to reduce the number of feral pigs that were running around the countryside in Dumfries and Galloway. It was a successful campaign and I think most of the hunters who took part enjoyed the experience, although it would be fair to say that some were unable to cope with the long, cold hours of vigilance that were required.

We had several sites that were baited and the technique was to sit in a high seat under a full moon and wait for the quarry to come in to eat. This did not always work sometimes the wild boar were simply not in the area or chose to dine at unattended bait sites. Quite often hunters would become disenchanted as the hours slipped by and the temperatures dropped without a wild boar putting in an appearance. Typically they would go to a blind at about 9.00pm and by 2.00am the cold would have taken its toll and the hunters would either call in to be collected or make their own way to the warmth and comfort of their hotel bed. These events were recorded on trail cameras and ironically the sites were quite often hit by the boar within an hour of the hunter giving up. The reasons given for leaving early were varied, but without a doubt, on a cold winter's night, the long vigil requires a good degree of determination.

In all though, those days of culling the free ranging population of wild boar in the area were successful and are indelibly etched in my memory.

The SCI entry form for trophy measurement

WILD PIGS OF THE WORLD

The pig is an animal in the genus *Sus*, and belonging to the *Suidae* family of even-toed ungulates. Pigs include the domestic pig and its ancestor, the common Eurasian wild boar, *Sus scrofa*; with *Sus* being the genus and *scrofa* being the species.

There are 17 species of pig that are recognized within the family *Suidae*, which in terms of evolution makes it a successful species that is ecologically versatile. Some of these species are however highly threatened with very few remaining animals in the wild.

The *Suidae* family can be easily recognised as pigs by the giveaway cartilaginous snout disc. This easily recognised feature has adapted to suit the pig's lifestyle of rooting in the soil, which is what other, less familiar species such as aardvarks and coatis use it for.

Pigs are small to medium size animals, with relatively large heads, short necks, small eyes and prominent ears. They are also typically stockily built with a bristly coat, and a short tail ending in a tassel.

They can be found in a great range of environments, from dense tropical rainforests to dry, open woodlands, grasslands and deserts; in fact, there seem to be few ecological conditions that pigs cannot cope with. Female wild pigs often live in large family groups, while the males tend to be solitary except during the rut.

The family *Suidae* are the only ungulates to commonly produce large numbers of offspring; litters of between one and six are normal. Infants of most species, with the exception of the babirusa and the warthogs, are marked with horizontal stripes, which provide camouflage especially in woodland areas.

Pigs are omnivores, highly social and intelligent animals. It will be no surprise to anyone who has studied them that they are usually rated fourth in overall intelligence, behind great apes, dolphins and elephants. They have sophisticated learning and problem solving abilities and it has been suggested that their intelligence is similar to that of a three-year-old human child.

As has already been mentioned, there are 17 species of wild pigs in the world and two or three are sufficiently different or iconic, such as the warthog, that they are worthy of special mention.

The slightly abbreviated scientific classification of pigs is as follows:

Kingdom: *Animalia*
Phylum: *Chordata*
Class: *Mammalia*
Order: *Artiodactyla*
Family: *Suidae*
Genus: *Sus*

Warthogs are prevalent across most of Africa

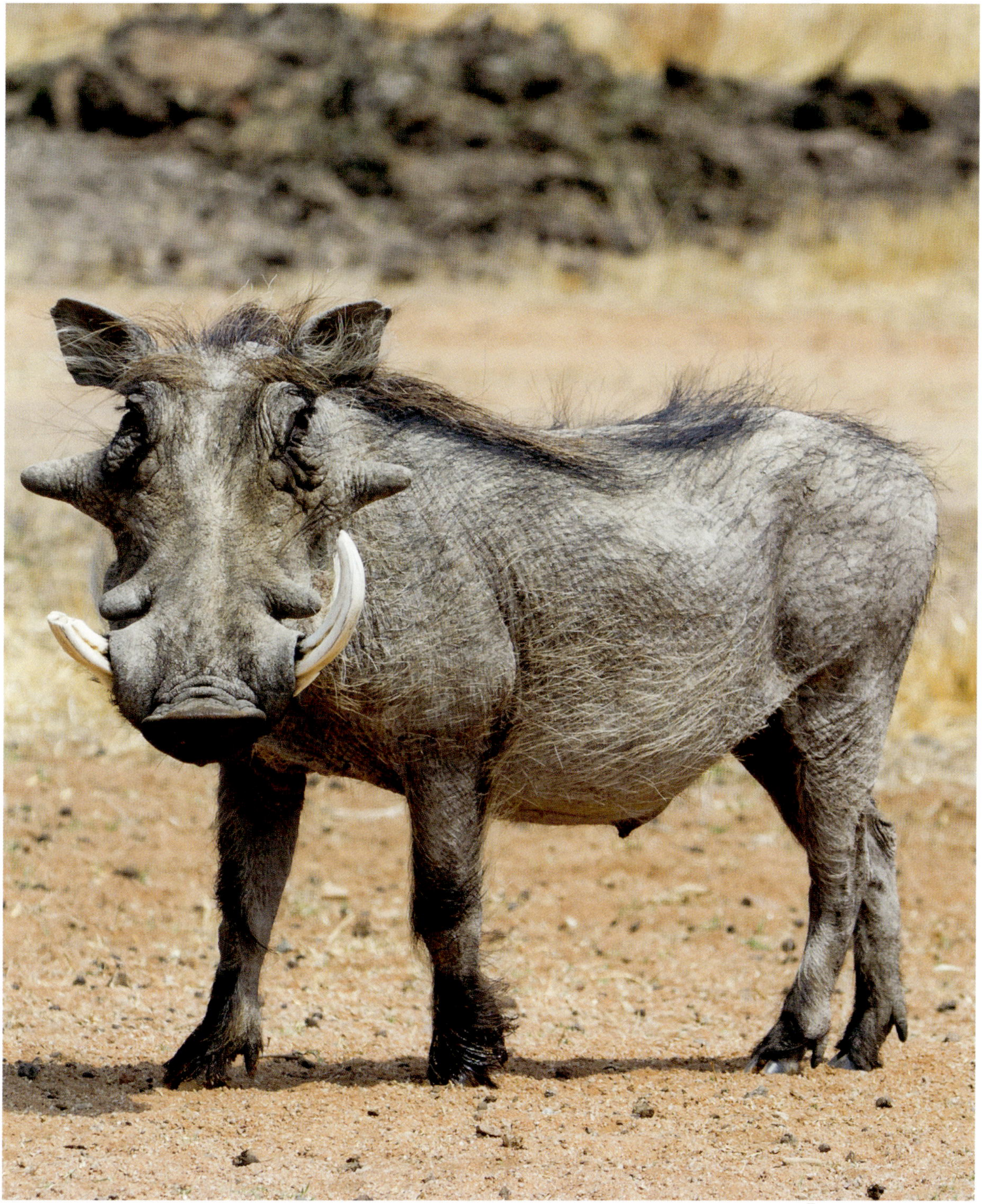

Chapter 7   WILD PIGS OF THE WORLD

The upper tusks in male warthogs measure, on average, between 25 and 30cm

Warthog

Warthogs are found over most of the African continent and have several different sub species. This pig measures between 125-150cm in length for the boar and 105-140cm for the sow. The average weight is around 85kg, with an adult male weighing as much as 150kg.

This pig has long legs and short neck. Proportionally it has a massive head with a broad and flattened muzzle and snout, and prominent curved tusks flaring upwards. The upper tusks measure an average 25-30 cm in length in adult males whereas the lower tusks are only 13 cm. The greyish body is barrel-shaped with a hairless skin that can take on differing hues of grey or brown depending on the colour of the soil in its wallows.

The dorsal mane of yellowish to jet black hairs is longest on the shoulders and neck. It has a narrow, tufted tail that is held vertically when trotting. Characteristically, many individuals sport whitish bristles on the lower jaw that forms conspicuous 'sideburns'. They can also look like large tusks at first glance.

The warthog has three pairs of facial 'warts' of different shape and thickness that are made of fibrous tissue and are situated on the muzzle, along the jaw, and under the eyes. In males, warts can grow up to 15 cm and have a protective function, and they are always conical. Warts, as well as tusks and preorbital glands are less developed in the female.

Common warthogs are often seen trotting in a quick, springy stride, with the head held high and the back rigid. When grazing or rooting, they often drop on their 'knees' instead of stretching their short neck.

They are the only African pigs that are an open-country species, with morphological and behavioural adaptations typical to grazers. Generally they are confined to various types of savannah grasslands, open bush lands and woodlands that are within range of a water hole. Although they are not usually found in forests, thickets, deserts and steppes, Common warthogs are present in arid lands near the Danakil desert and Bale Mountains forests.

The number of warthogs in an area is likely to be proportional to the aardvark population, as warthogs need deep burrows for protection from predators as well as from variations in temperature and humidity. Aardvark holes provide just such protection. While their body can

Warthogs can be easily identified by the eponymous warts on their face

obviously tolerate heat up to a point, they cope with high temperature by sheltering into shade, wallowing and dust-bathing. Piglets are particularly vulnerable to cold and malnutrition during drought, which, together with predation and other factors, account for over 50 per cent of mortalities during the first year.

Common warthogs have an omnivorous diet, which is similar to most pigs. Their diet is composed largely of grasses, roots, fruits, bark, fungi, eggs, carrions, as well as small mammals, reptiles and birds. Areas with abundant food resources like bulbs, rhizomes and nutritious roots can sustain large numbers of animals. They are powerful diggers, using both snout and hooves, but not tusks.

When feeding, they often move around walking on their anterior knuckles with their hindquarters raised. They use their incisors to wrench grass stems or strip seed heads, and they excavate rhizomes and mineral-rich earth with the hard edge of their snout.

Common warthogs are highly diurnal. They go underground before dark and sleep in abandoned burrows of aardvarks or other animals. Males enter last and commonly reverse in, with the head facing the opening, and ready to fight an intruder or rush out as needed.

Their daytime activity includes a range of typical occupations like feeding, drinking, wallowing, rubbing against trees or termite mounds, and grooming. Feeding occurs mainly in early morning and late afternoon, but they also graze between periods of resting in the shade of bushy thickets or in mud wallows.

Bushpigs

These are another African member of the *Suidae* family and are of a similar size to the warthog, albeit a totally different shape. They are usually between 130-190cm long and on average weigh in at about 85kg.

Bushpigs have a compact body with short legs, rounded back and elongated snout. Their coat is extremely variable in colour, ranging from blond, up to a dark brown or near-black. Colour may vary with sex, age, region or individual, but generally it has a paler head with white face markings. The body hairs are long and sparse, but are elongated between the forehead and the tail, forming a white or greyish dorsal crest. It has a long tufted tail. Piglets are dark brown in colour with longitudinal stripes or rows of lighter spots.

This species, like the other pigs, is omnivorous and highly adaptable. It is probably a major seed disperser. Bushpigs consume roots, tubers, bulbs, corn, fungi, fruit, eggs, invertebrates, birds, small mammals, and carrion.

In some parts of Africa, bushpigs have been seen following groups of monkeys as they forage and feed on discarded fruits. As with other members of the suidae family bush pigs make extensive use of their snout to rummage for larvae, worms and underground root systems.

Rooting carried out by bushpigs can leave large areas of ploughed up ground clear of standing vegetation. In cultivated areas, sounders can do serious damage to crops in a short time.

The bush pig is very similar in appearance to the red river hog. In areas where they are both found the bush pig tends to favour higher altitudes, whereas the bush pig will inhabit the lowland forests. In other areas the species are separated by geographical barriers, such as the River Congo. Bushpigs frequent a wide range of forested habitats, from sea level to as high as 4,000m on Mount Kilimanjaro, although they show a marked preference for valley bottoms with soft soils and dense vegetation.

Bushpigs have an elongated snout and white facial markings

WILD BOAR – A BRITISH PERSPECTIVE

Chapter 7 **WILD PIGS OF THE WORLD**

The bushpig is predominantly nocturnal, resting under heavy thickets of vegetation during the day. In the cooler parts of their range, for example in the southern Cape of South Africa, they tend to be more diurnal during the colder months, suggesting that temperature regulation is a significant factor influencing their rhythm of activity.

Population density is regulated by a wide range of predators, including man, lions, leopards, spotted hyenas, pythons and eagles. They are courageous and dangerous when cornered, with both boars and sows aggressively defending their litters if threatened.

Bushpigs run fast and swim easily and their sense of smell and hearing is very good, but their eyesight is only fair. They live in family sounders of six to 12, led by a dominant male. Contrary to other wild pigs, adult males play an active role in rearing and defending the young. Other males are aggressively chased off and territorial defence is characterised by ritualised displays and scent marking.

Males disperse from the sounder as they reach sexual maturity and old males become solitary, whereas females by and large remain on their home range.

Bushpigs are not listed on CITES and are classified as of 'least concern" on the IUCN Red List due to the species being widespread and common.

Babirusa pig

There are three species of babirusa. The Togian babirusa is the largest as well as being the rarest. It has sparser, shorter body hair than the Moluccan babirusa and, in contrast to the Sulawesi babirusa, the tail tuft is well developed.

The upper canines of males are these species' most distinctive features: they

Above: The Sulawesi babirusa, a rare member of the Suidae family

Left: The red river hog (Potamochoerus porcus), which is also know as a bush pig, is not to be confused with the bushpig (Potamochoerus larvatus)

WILD BOAR – A BRITISH PERSPECTIVE   137

Chapter 7 — WILD PIGS OF THE WORLD

Babirusas are distinguishable by their upward curving and converging upper canines

are short, slender, rotated forwards and always converge.

Genetic studies suggest that babirusas diverged from other pigs during the Miocene period, which was between 10 and 19 million years ago. This could also have been the time that they became isolated on the Indonesian island of Sulawesi.

All three babirusa come from the islands of Indonesia and inhabit the tropical rainforests and the banks of rivers and ponds. Another common trait in all three species is that they are extremely rare.

Much of what is known about the Togian babirusa comes from anecdotal evidence that has been given by natives of the island. It is regarded as an endangered species and its numbers are continuing to decline.

The Moluccan babyrusa is a relatively smaller cousin of the Togian species. It is covered in long thick body hair and has a well-developed tail tuft. Locals on the island of Buru report that the babirusas feed primarily on leaves, roots and fruits of the forest, but never raid cultivated crops unlike other species of pig on the island that cause considerable damage.

They are reported to be mostly solitary or may occasionally be seen in small groups generally in the early morning or late afternoon. Nothing is known about the breeding habits of the species, which is red on the IUCN list of endangered animals. They are so rare that in 1995 no evidence could be found of its continued existence although locals claim that it is still to be found.

There is some evidence that the Sulawesi babirusa is closely related to the Togian animal, but in the absence of specimens the theory cannot be put to the test.

WILD BOAR – A BRITISH PERSPECTIVE

WILD BOAR RECIPES

The wild boar recipes in this section of the book are ones that I have collected and tried over the years and are recipes for meals that I have found particularly enjoyable. I have no idea of the origins of most of them; they have simply been scribbled down in a notebook and quite often added to or altered in some way to appeal to my, or my guests', taste.

When cooking wild boar it is best to treat it as though it is a game meat rather than pork, which of course it is not. All animal muscle is made up of both red and white fibres, therefore a typical red meat, beef for example, will have by far and away more red fibres than white. Domestically raised pork on the other hand will have more white fibres than red in the ratio of 20 per cent red to 80 per cent white, hence the colour of the meat.

Wild boar is the other way around, where the structure of the meat is in the ratio of 70 per cent to 30 per cent in favour of the red fibres. For this reason the texture is different to pork as well, in fact it looks and feels on the palate more like beef or perhaps a little like venison. Wild boar is generally a lean meat, or should I say it is perceived as being lean because the fat tends to be stored under the skin in a layer as opposed to being marbled through the muscle as in the aforementioned beef. This is convenient because it can be cut off if all that is required is a juicy lean steak or cutlet, or it can be utilised for basting. Many connoisseurs would argue that it is actually more succulent than the meat itself. Wild boar fat is mainly unsaturated and although I have never tried it, I understand that it makes the most delicious crackling.

Apple sauce traditionally accompanies pork and it goes well with wild boar too, but make sure that you at least try it with redcurrant jelly or cranberry jelly as well.

Wines to drink with wild boar

Now I must confess right from the start that I am no wine buff, and I am quite certain that readers of this treatise will be every bit of a sommelier as me, if not more, so I felt that I owed it to my readers to do a modicum of research into the subject.

However, I also decided that for the wild boar virgin, that poor unfortunate soul who has never been blessed with savouring the delight of a meal of wild boar, I should make my own preference of wine known for no other reason than that I enjoy the combination so much that I am sure there must be at least one other person out there that would feel the same way. I must admit, though, as far as the wines are concerned, my choice is largely because I enjoy them and would drink them anyway, not because of some gastronomic insight into what wine is best suited to wild boar.

Top tips for cooking wild boar

A wild boar could live as long as 30 years of age in captivity, but believe me you would not want to eat it. As the animal ages so its flavour develops, but regrettably so does its toughness. An older animal really is only any good for burgers and sausages, but I must say it does that very well. If you do choose to cook a more mature animal you will need to marinade for four or five days, ideally using pineapple juice, which is a great tenderiser and maybe consider a slowly cooked casserole.

Where possible go for an animal that is between 10 and 16 months old.

When considering a marinade go for herbs such as rosemary, tarragon and bay. It should also be well larded, either from fat trimmings or by using pork fat, to ensure the meat doesn't become dry.

Be careful not to use a wine marinade for a long period on young meat due to its propensity to turn the flesh a purple colour.

Ensure that young meat does not dry out during cooking by basting frequently.

In order to eliminate the very small risk (if it is home-grown wild boar) of *trichinella* infection, make sure that the meat is cooked thoroughly. This is the same advice as would be given for the cooking of pork.

My own choice then, in order of preference, and for that matter price, is a Nuits-St-Georges, followed by a Châteauneuf-du-Pape, and last, but not necessarily least, a Côtes du Rhône. All three are French wines, the first from Burgundy, while the other two are from the Rhone region of the country. All of them are red, which fits the stereotypical choice of red wine for red meat. In the case of game meat, however, there is probably a good reason for choosing red wine because, without meaning to sound pretentious, I think that a full bodied fruity wine is needed to complement the strong taste of the meat.

Imagine my surprise then, when I embarked upon my research, to discover that the wine merchants and importers Alexander Hadleigh agreed with me. Well at least they immediately suggested a Châteauneuf-du-Pape, and so I felt one out of three was not doing too badly.

Berry Bros. and Rudd recommended a Beaujolais Crus, a decision based apparently upon the need to avoid too high a tannin count. This information went above my head, but I consoled myself with thinking that a Beaujolais is not too far adrift from my personal choices. My only concern with Messrs Berry Bros. and Rudd's advice was that I felt that they were likening wild boar to pork rather too much.

Other red wines that came highly recommended were Shiraz, an Australian name, which in its country of origin, France, is known as Syrah, and two wines from Italy, Barlo and Brunello, as well as another French wine, Pinot Noir. I was also delighted to learn that several more informed opinions agreed with my choice of the Côtes du Rhône.

For those readers that prefer a white wine, I understand from my investigations that a Pinot Blanc and Chardonnay are extremely acceptable as accompaniments to wild boar.

My ramblings on wine are not meant to be extensive or definitive, just me passing on a pleasurable dining experience for the reader to try and to reach his own conclusions.

Chapter 8: WILD BOAR RECIPES

Wild Boar Casserole

Serves 6
3lbs of diced wild boar
6oz of trimmed boar fat/butter
2lbs of onion
3 cloves of garlic (optional)
3oz flour
Parsley or thyme
1 pint cider
Salt and pepper

Chop and fry the onions (add the garlic at this point if required) in a large frying pan using half the fat until a golden colour. Remove and place to one side. Roll the diced meat in flour and, using the remaining fat, fry quickly to seal. Put a layer of onions in the bottom of a casserole dish and add the parsley or thyme and then add a layer of meat. Then add another layer of onions and meat. Repeat, finishing with a layer of meat. Pour the cider into the dish, season and bring to the boil. Cover the dish and cook in a moderate oven (180°C) for three hours.

Cutlets of Wild Boar with Morello Cherries

Serves 4
4 decent-sized wild boar cutlets, 10-12oz each
For the wine marinade
300ml full bodied red wine
1 shallot, peeled and sliced
1 tablespoon balsamic vinegar
1 fresh bay leaf
1 tablespoon muscovado sugar
6 juniper berries
1 clove of garlic, peeled
2 allspice berries
For the morello sauce
1 tablespoon dried morello cherries
125g stoned fresh morello cherries soaked in 5 tablespoons of red wine
½ stick of cinnamon
Salt and pepper
2 tablespoons of wild fruit jelly

First we have to marinade the meat. Trim the excess fat from the meat and rub it with salt. Then bring the ingredients of the marinade to the boil and simmer for 15 minutes in a non-stick saucepan. Wipe the excess salt from the meat and cover with the cooled marinade. Keep covered in the refrigerator for 48 hours.

Heat a little oil or trimmed wild boar fat in a heavy, deep frying pan. Drain and dry the meat, discarding the marinade. Sear the cutlets quickly in a hot pan over a high temperature, then gently fry for about 10 minutes on each side until nicely browned. Cover the pan and continue to cook the cutlets in their own juices over the lowest possible heat until tender, which will probably be another 30–40 minutes depending on thickness. Meanwhile simmer the soaked cherries and cinnamon gently in the wine for about five minutes then strain, separately reserving the cherries and the wine.

Transfer the cooked meat to a plate, cover and place in a warm oven. Deglaze the frying pan with the wine, scraping any sediment into the stock. Add the stock and reduce, stirring until the sauce becomes syrupy. Strain through a fine sieve into a fresh saucepan, add the reserved cherries and a little wild fruit jelly and season to taste. Add any fresh, cooked cherries to the sauce, heat thorough and transfer the cutlets and sauce to a hot serving dish.

The cutlets will become more succulent for 15-20 minutes resting. If making the dish in advance, cool the cooked cutlets and sauce quickly and store in the refrigerator, reheating gently to serve.

Wild Boar Steaks on Sauerkraut

Serves 6
12 wild boar steaks, 4oz each
1 bay leaf
1 chopped onion
1 large potato, grated finely
4oz trimmed boar fat
2oz flour
1lb sauerkraut
1 pint hot stock
1/8 pint white vinegar
1/4 pint white wine
Salt and pepper
1/2 teaspoon of sugar
2 juniper berries

Sauté the onion in a little oil in a saucepan. Add the trimmed fat and cook a little longer, then add the sauerkraut, vinegar and wine. Season with the sugar, juniper berries and bay leaf. Bring to the boil, then stir in the grated potato and return to the boil until the sauerkraut thickens. Remove from the heat and reheat when required.

Heat a heavy bottomed frying pan and sauté the steaks until done, which will be about 15 minutes. Remove the steaks and add the flour to the pan. Cook for a few minutes then add the hot stock, stirring constantly. Bring to the boil.

Dress the steaks on the sauerkraut and coat with the sauce to serve.

Honeyed Haunch of Wild Boar

Serves 6
1 whole haunch of wild boar
Vegetable stock
3oz of trimmed wild boar fat
6 tablespoons of honey
Salt and pepper
2 tablespoons of all of the following: juniper berries, Worcestershire sauce, currants, mint and cumin

Remove any surface fat from the haunch and seal the meat in a frying pan. Then place the haunch on some silver foil and spread the trimmed fat all over the meat. Season the meat and add the Worcestershire sauce followed by the honey. Finally spread the berries and herbs all over the meat. Fold the foil up sufficiently to contain a half pint of the stock and then seal the foil. Cook in a gentle oven, gas mark 3-4 or equivalent, for four hours or until the meat falls from the bone. Baste every hour.

INDEX

ACCURACY 76-80, 86, 98-99
AFTER THE SHOT 93
ANGLO-SAXON 19-23
ANIMAL WELFARE ACT 52
ARDWINNA 19
ARTHUR, KING 19-20
AT FORCE HUNTING 23
AXTEN, TERRY 120

BABIRUSA 130, 137-138
BAILEY, LUCKY 64
BALLISTIC COEFFICIENT 62, 64
BALLISTIC TIPS 66
BALLISTICS 57-58, 64, 66
BARKER, ROGER 113
BATTLE OF HASTINGS 20, 32
BEAKER PEOPLE 16
BEDDING RIFLE BARRELS 84, 98
BEHAVIOUR 37
BELL, WALTER 'KARAMOJO' 58
BERN CONVENTION 31
BLAIR, TONY 105
BOADICEA 18
BOLT ACTION RIFLES 56, 68-71, 76-87
BOW AND STABLE HUNTING 23-24
BRENNEKE 68
BULLET DROP 61, 65, 74-75
BURNS INQUIRY/ REPORT 105
BUSHPIG 134-137

CALIBRES 57
CARMINNOWS SPORTING ESTATE 120-122
CELTS 14, 18
CHASING AWAY 108-109
CHROMOSOME 34
CLASSIFICATION, PIGS 130
CLEANING, THE WEAPON 96-97
CLEAVES 49
CRANMER, THOMAS 27
CULHWCH 19-20

DANGEROUS WILD ANIMALS ACT 1976 .... 28, 52
DEFRA 30-33, 66, 106, 108-109
DENTITION 43

DEW CLAWS 49
DIANA 19, 52
DIET 41-44, 134
DNA 34
DOGS, HUNTING WITH 23, 103-109
DOMESDAY BOOK 20-21
DOUBLE RIFLES 57, 68, 70-71
DOUBLE SET TRIGGERS 114-117
DRAG HUNT 108-109
DRILLING RIFLE 68, 71

ELIZABETH I 24-25, 28
EPPING FOREST 23, 27
EXEMPT HUNTING 108-109
EXIT PUPIL 72-74
EXTINCTION OF WILD BOAR IN BRITAIN 19, 28
EYE RELIEF 72, 75, 103

FARMING, WILD BOAR 28
FARROWING 39-40
FERAL WILD BOAR 30, 32, 129
FIELD OF VIEW 72-74
FIREARM LAW 66
FOOTPRINTS 49
FOREST LAWS 21-23, 27
FOREST OF DEAN 20, 23, 31

GESTATION 39
GLANDS, LACHRYMAL 40
GODWINSON, HAROLD 20
GOULDING, MARTIN 55
GRALLOCH 94
GRAND GRIFFON VENDÉEN 110
GRAY, JOHN 33

HABITAT 42
HALSTEAD, ELIZABETH 40
HARMS, SIMON 120
HART 21-26
HEARING 35, 100
HENRY II 21
HENRY VIII 24-28
HIGGINS, LARRY 119
HIGH SEAT 51-53, 56, 93, 101, 112-114, 122-123

HOME RANGE	38
HUNTER-GATHERER	14-16
ILLEGAL HUNTING	106, 108-109
IRON AGE PIGS	28
JOHNSON, SID & JERRY	128
JOHNSTON, ANDREW	30
KINETIC ENERGY	57-60
LABRADOR	110
LAIE MENEUSE	90
LARGE BLACK PIG	37
LEFORS, JOE	50
LOCK TIME	98
MABINOGI, FABLES	19
MAMMAL SOCIETY	31
MANNERS	56
MARCUM, RALPH	113
MATING	38-40
MCCRAVE, MIKE	117
MEAT, CUTS OF	95
MERLIN	20
MIRE	44
MODERATORS	100
MOMENTUM	57-59, 63-64
MONTAGUE, LORD	26
MUZZLE BRAKE	99
MYTHOLOGY	18
NEW FOREST	23
NOSLER, JOHN	59
OBJECTIVE LENS	72-74
OESTRUS	28, 37-39, 91, 119, 121
OPTICS	71
PACE, RICHARD	21
PACE, BYRON	91
PARALLAX	75
PARTITION BULLET	59, 66
PHOTOPERIODISM	39
POINT BLANK RANGE	61
POSITIONS, SHOOTING	101
RECIPES	142
RECOIL	99
RED DOT SCOPES	75
REPRODUCTION	38-40
RETICLE	74

RETURN TO THE WILD	30
RIFLE REVIEWS	76-87
RIFLES	68
ROMANS	14-16, 24
ROYAL GREEN JACKET	64
RUST	97
SACKMAN, BARBARA	112
SAFETY	56
SAFETY CATCH	57, 78-79
SCHOLES, LYNDON	117-126
SEERAD	30
SHOT PLACEMENT	92
SHOTGUNS	57, 66-71
SKARA BRAE	16
SMOKING	101
SNIPER	59, 64, 103
SOUNDER	37,-41, 50, 53-54, 90, 120, 124, 137
SPOT AND STALK	51-52, 56
ST HUBERT	52
ST HUBERT HOUND	110
STAG	23, 25-26, 54, 105
STALKING STICKS	99
TAMWORTHS	28
TEKKEL	107
TERRIER, GERMAN HUNTING	107
TESTOSTERONE	39
TOWNIE VOTE	105
TRACKING	20, 38, 50
TRAJECTORY	60
TRICHINELLA SPIRALIS	30
TRIGGERS	56-58, 98
TUDORS	28
TURBERVILLE, GEORGE	25
TWENTIETH LEGION	18
TWRCH TRWYTH	19
UNINTENTIONAL HUNTING	109
VENERIE, NOBLE ART OF	25
VISION	74
WALLOWING	51, 134
WARTHOG	130-134
WEIGHT	30-45
WILD MAMMALS (PROTECTION) ACT	52, 109
WILLIAM THE CONQUEROR	21, 32
WINDAGE	62
WINE	140-141

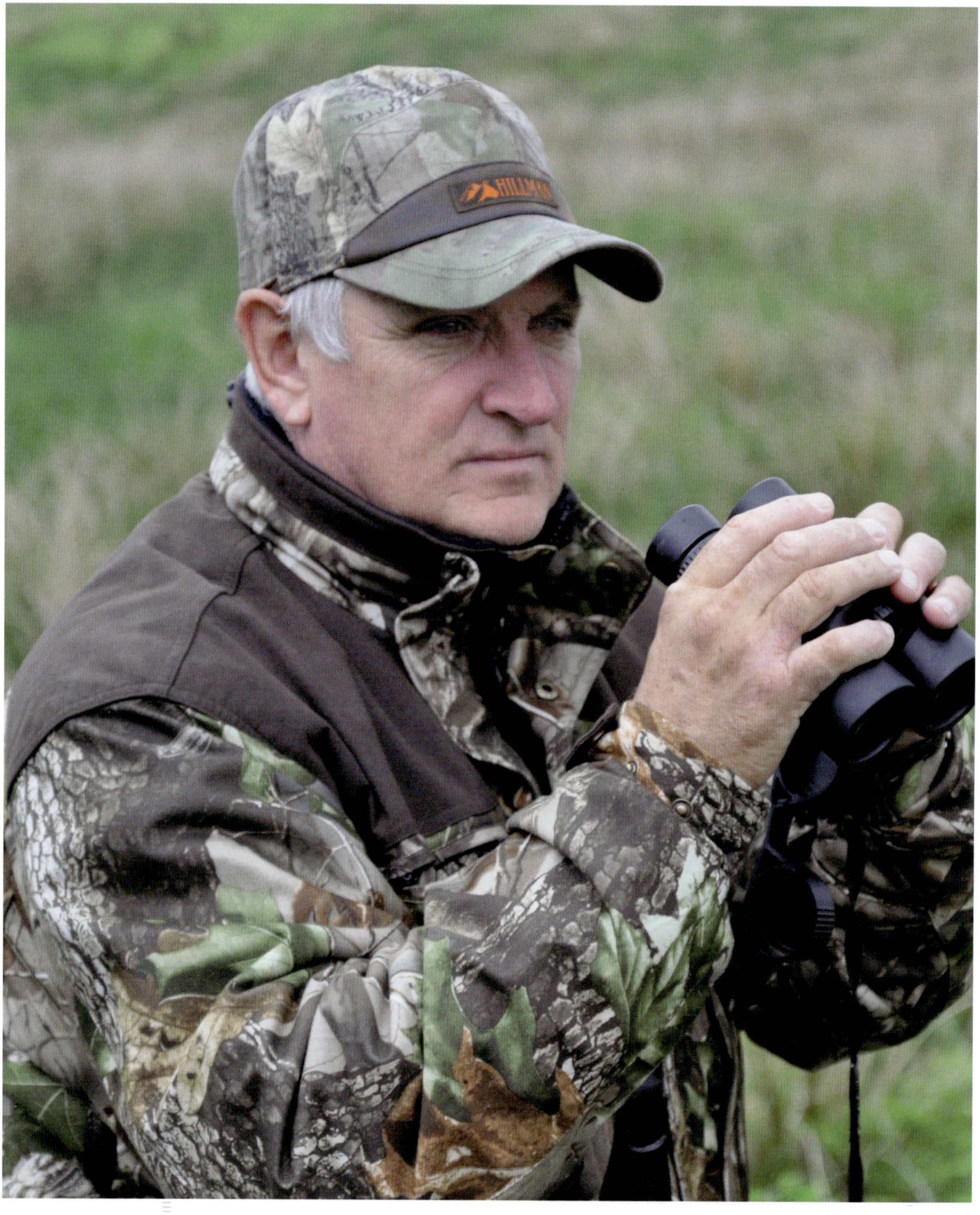

ABOUT THE AUTHOR

Steve Sweeting was born in east London, but at a very early age moved to Epping in Essex, where he lived until his early 20s.

From an early age he used to treat Epping Forest as his personal playground, and it was here that he began learning about wildlife, often spending days at a time sleeping in crudely made bivouacs fashioned from natural materials found in the woods and watching and tracking the deer. In those days the deer in Epping Forest were almost exclusively fallow.

As a boy he befriended gamekeepers on local estates and spent much of his spare time helping them go about their duties.

He was educated at Epping Secondary School, and then at Turnford College in Hertfordshire where he applied to London University to study veterinary medicine. He was offered a place, although at the last minute did not accept and went into the pharmaceutical industry instead.

Since he can remember Steve has been passionate about hunting and firearms and spent one part of his life serving in the TAVR as a volunteer soldier, which seemed to satisfy both interests.

For a number of years he was the chairman of an Essex based Rifle and Pistol club, is qualified as a range conducting officer and is still a registered firearm dealer. Until recently he owned a sporting estate in Scotland where he now lives. He still farms both wild boar and deer.

Steve is a prodigious hunter and spent many years selling hunts to individuals and parties within the Safari Club International organisation, primarily to American clients.

For the last 15 years Steve has organised hunting expeditions worldwide, specialising in the Americas and Africa as well as here at home.

ACKNOWLEDGEMENTS

Andrew Johnston of Hilton Wild Boar for his input and advice over a good many years.

Allan Smith (professional photographer), who has patiently tutored me in both the art and science of his profession as well as putting the finishing touches to the illustrations in this book.

Lyndon Scholes for keeping the wheels turning on the farm while I hid away with my word processor; and for his efforts as my cartoonist.

Peter Carr for his words of wisdom in writing the foreword.

Thanks to Jane Winters at the Institute of Historical Research, John Gray of DEFRA (Scotland), and DEFRA for their help.

REFERENCES

Alison Weir (2001) *Henry VIII The King and his Court*.

Arthur F Kinney et al (2000) *Tudor England, An Encyclopaedia*.

Robert A. Rinker (1999) *Understanding Firearm Ballistics*.

Jim Barrington at The All Party Parliamentary Middle Way Group, Hunting With Dogs paper.